KOREAN KUNG FU

The Chinese Connection

KOREAN KUNG FU

The Chinese Connection

UPDATED AND EXPANDED EDITION

BY JAMES THEROS

KOREAN KUNG FU: THE CHINESE CONNECTION
(Updated and expanded edition)
Copyright ©2014 James Theros

All rights reserved. Printed in the United States of America. No part of this book may be used or reproduced in any manner whatsoever without written permission from the author.

Copies of this book may be purchased for educational, business, or sales promotional use.

For information please write or email:
Level 10 Publishing,
5135 S. Emerson Ave. Suite B.
Indianapolis, IN 46237
lion@level10martialarts.com

Photos by Debi Theros, Charles Edmonds and Saul Easley, Ashley Furgason
Book design by Sue Balcer of JustYourType.biz

UPDATED AND EXPANDED EDITION

Library of Congress Cataloging-in-Publication Data
Korean Kung Fu: The Chinese Connection,
    James Theros—2nd ed.

ISBN 978-0-9904164-0-1

The text in this book was set in Utopia.

Contents

Chapter 1. My Story 1

Chapter 2. Kung Fu 17

Chapter 3. Korean Kung Fu 21

Chapter 4. History of Korean Kung Fu 31

Chapter 5. Meditation 47

Chapter 6. Energy Development 53

Chapter 7. The 8-Section Brocade 57

Chapter 8. Tai Chi Quan 67

Chapter 9. Basic Kung Fu Stances 91

Chapter 10 TanTui 95

Chapter 11. Iron Body Conditioning 113

Chapter 12. 2-Man Training 119

Chapter 13. Forms Training 129

Chapter 14. So Chu Kwon 141

Chapter 15. Ag Ga Kwon 157

Chapter 16 Mei Hwa Kwon 165

Contents

Chapter 17. Kum Gang Kwon 181

Chapter 18. So Ho Yun Kwon 193

Chapter 19. My Teachers 213

Chapter 20. Interview with Grandmaster Na Hi-Seup 243

Chapter 21. Interview with Master Choi Bok-Kyu 269

Chapter 22. Interview with Grandmaster James Cook 283

Chapter 23. Interview with Grandmaster Seo Myung Won 295

Chapter 24. Interview with Seo Jin-Woo 301

Chapter 25. The Future of Korean Kung Fu 307

Chapter 26. Reference Chart & Korean Alphabet 311

           Conclusion 321

           Acknowledgements 335

KOREAN KUNG FU

The Chinese Connection

Chapter One

My Story

I began my training in 1976 in an Okinawan art called Shorin Ryu Karate at my 2nd grade elementary school in an afterschool enrichment program. I then enrolled in a Shorei Goju Ryu/Judo school in 1982, but my mother did not want to pay the tuition so I had to stop attending there within the first several months of training.

In 1983 I was fortunate enough to live right across the street from where a new master had just opened his school.

One look at him and I immediately knew that I was going to join his school. He looked very much like a Korean version of Jackie Chan, and he was wearing a peach-colored Chinese Kung Fu uniform. In the image below, take note that Grandmaster Choi is wearing his peach-colored Kung Fu uniform, and there is a chinese scroll and a Chinese broad sword on the wall, but the guy in the background is wearing a standard white Karate uniform.

Grandmaster Young Pyo Choi 1983

I trained with Master Choi from 1983 – 2003 in the arts of Tae Kwon Do/Tang Soo Do (the art that he originally taught when I joined was called, "Korean Karate"--otherwise known as Tang Soo Do) and around 1995 he began replacing the forms and self-defense techniques from Tang Soo Do to the WTF Olympic Tae Kwon Do curriculum (replacing the Pyung Ahn forms with the Tae Geuk forms, but keeping all of the black belt Tang Soo Do forms, while only adding specific WTF black belt TKD forms for competition reasons).

I also received training in Hapkido with Grandmaster Choi; since the vast majority of our self-defense skills were Hapkido techniques, and I learned many additional Hapkido skills and techniques at our 4 annual training camps held each year in Ohio.

Those arts were wonderful beginnings for me, but my most prized training came by getting the privilege of learning Grandmaster Choi's Korean Kung Fu system.

He ran the Kung Fu classes during the afternoons and the Tae Kwon Do classes in the evenings. The afternoon classes were always very small in comparison to the evening classes, so I always received very good personal training from Grandmaster Choi, being that I was one of his first students when he arrived in Indianapolis.

Eventually, he moved the Kung Fu classes to late evenings (8:30-10pm) and I enjoyed a lot of late-night chats with Grandmaster Choi after practices ended, which I always treasured.

In 2003, I made a decision to form my own personal organization, to have the opportunity to implement some changes to my school at the time. My school had just been hit by

Chapter 1. MY STORY

a tornado and destroyed, and I was going through a lot of personal challenges at that time. I did my very best to try and work things out between us and I tried diligently to keep a relationship with him.

For 10 years, I continued to send him birthday cards, father's day cards and Christmas cards, but, alas, he is still upset that I left his organization. At the time, I was his highest-ranking student, and I had trained with him for 20 years; so I'm sure that it must have really hurt him when I made the move, and probably left him feeling a bit embarrassed that someone who had trained with him for so long would leave his organization, leaving him to explain to others why his top student (and owner of one of his branch schools) would seemingly just *up and leave.*

When I left I needed to find someplace to continue my training. I researched every master that I could find who had similar arts to the ones I had spent the past 20 years learning, and I flew out and met many of these masters in person. I tried a few places out before eventually finding my new home.

One of the people that I first contacted had a website that had lots of familiar content on it, and the big selling point for me was that he taught the same Kung Fu system that I had learned. There was quite a bit of information on the website and, though I recognized many of the forms, there were still quite a few others that I did not recognize.

So, I contacted this master and got him to agree to allow me to fly out and meet with him to train. Prior to that time I had tried unsuccessfully for 2 years to get him to respond to an email, and I could never get an answer when I attempted to call.

Anyhow, I flew out to Riverside, California to meet and train with this Master (or so I thought).

When I arrived, he and his son met me at the airport and took me to get checked in at a hotel. After I got checked in, he proceeded to drive me to Los Angeles and other surrounding areas, showing me the various schools in that area that he knew about where Kung Fu was taught, and two schools that he believed were teaching Sip Pal Gi.

Then, he told me that he would introduce me to a new friend of his who had just come from Korea and had recently opened a Korean Kung Fu school in the Riverside area. He told me that this man had strictly trained in Kung Fu and had no Tae Kwon Do or Tang Soo Do training, which meant that I would be learning "pure" Kung Fu.

When we arrived, I was formally introduced to Grandmaster Hi Seup Na, and after talking with me briefly about my training, he began working with me on an advanced Kung Fu form that I had not previously learned. He *really* took me through the paces that day. Unfortunately, he would not allow me to take a picture with him, or allow me to film any of the training that day (standard fare for many Kung Fu masters) and when we finished the training, he would not allow me to film him performing the form he had just taught me, so the man who introduced me to him took me out to a local park and filmed me performing the form so I would have some way to continue practicing it once I returned to Indiana.

I somehow offended Grandmaster Na while I was training with him, and the master who introduced me to him told me that Grandmaster Na didn't want to train me any longer.

Chapter 1. MY STORY

Grandmaster Hi Seup Na Circa 2005

I was completely devastated. I had searched long and hard for so long and I had now finally found exactly what I was looking for!

I certainly had no intention of saying or doing anything that would turn him off; and I had no idea what it was that turned him off. In fact, I'm still not sure exactly what it was, but, my best guess is that he didn't like my *up-front American attitude*.

Anyhow, after that single day of training (we trained for 6 hours non-stop), I knew I had finally found "the holy grail" of this system, but, now I was left to find another way around the situation.

The master who was the go-between between Grandmaster Na and I told me that he, himself, no longer taught the art (due to health problems he was experiencing), so he wouldn't be able to help me. Little did he realize, though, he actually helped me a great deal that weekend.

After a trip to Chinatown in Los Angeles, the master took me back to the airport and we parted ways.

I had taken note of both of the schools that he took me to in the Los Angeles area, and when I returned to Indianapolis I began researching these schools.

To my great surprise, I couldn't find either of the schools online (this was 2003 and search engines were still fairly unreliable), so I booked another flight out to Los Angeles and physically went to visit both of these schools.

The first school that I visited was located on the East side of Los Angeles and they were very happy to see me. The master (a very nice lady and her husband) invited me to come and train with them and learn a form, but wanted to charge me $5,000 to learn a single form!

Unfortunately, she had an emergency come up and was not able to get back to the school to work with me; she had to leave while I was training on my own at her school, and I was left with a couple of her students.

I waited for a bit, hoping that she would return, but, after a few hours, I finally grew impatient and I left. I remembered the other location that this master had told me about, located in Koreatown, which wasn't too far from the school I had just visited.

I found the phone number in the local phone book and called. A Korean man answered and I inquired if he taught Sip Pal Gi. He informed me that he did, indeed, teach the art. I rattled off a few names of our forms and he immediately told me that they taught these forms, which excited me because I

Chapter 1. MY STORY

knew that if they taught these particular forms that the system would be very similar to the training that I had already received. I jumped in my car and sped over to Koreatown to visit the school.

I walked in and met Grandmaster Choi Byung Yil who was alone at the school at the time. His English was not great, so I think he appreciated the fact that I knew how to speak some Korean.

Grandmaster Byong Yil Choi, 2003

I began asking him about his system and threw some names of Kung Fu forms at him. He recognized all of them and told me that this was the same system that he taught here at his school. He was very gracious with me and he even gave me several documents that I still have in my possession.

Korean Kung Fu: The Chinese Connection

School Brochure

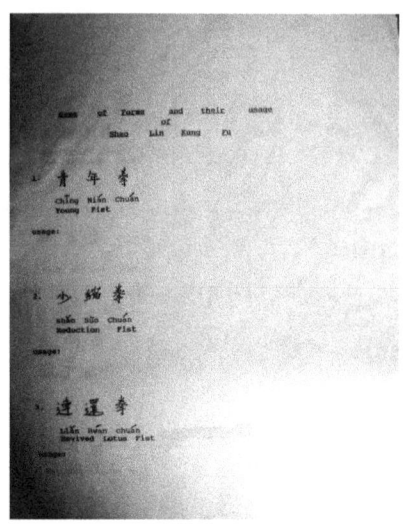

Form Translations

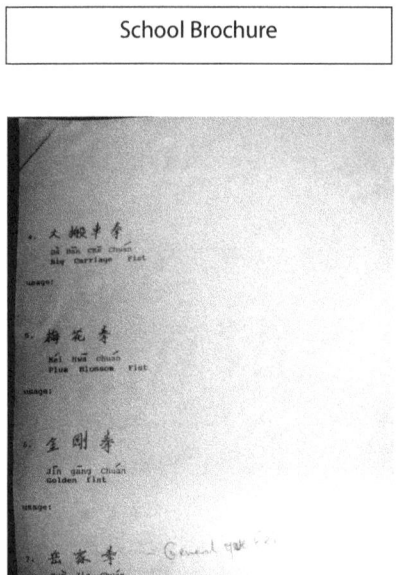

Form Translations

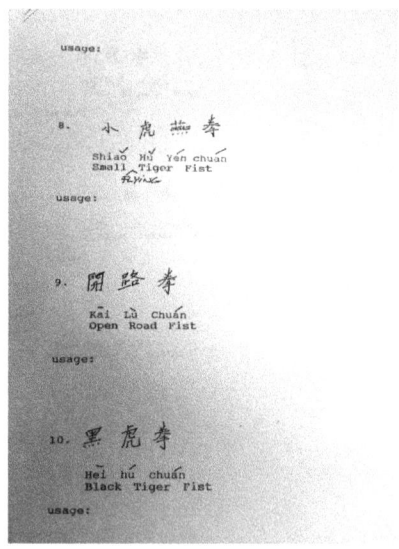

Form Translations

Chapter 1. MY STORY

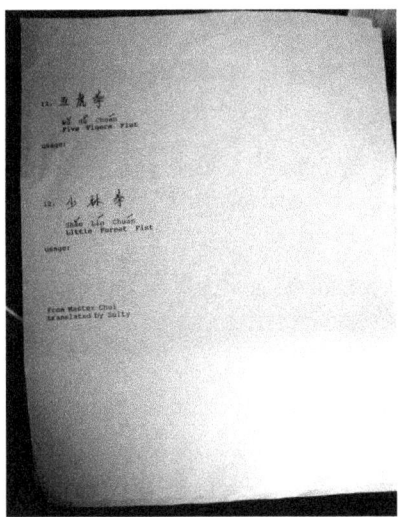

Form Translations

I talked with him for what seemed to be about an hour, and then ran out to the nearest bank and withdrew some cash to pay for a year's membership at his school, and I attended my first class with him that evening. I demonstrated some of my forms and weapons for his students and they demonstrated a few things for me as well.

I was very fortunate to find the school and I had no idea just how important finding that school was at the time.

I began flying out each month (sometimes twice) for 4 to 5 days each time and I trained at Master Choi's Koreatown school. There were Korean monks who lived above the school and their monastery was linked to the building that the school was in, so I would frequently see the monks, dressed in their gray robes, walking past the training room, and I would continually hear conversations in Korean between the monks (who would often stop in to speak with Grandmaster Choi), and Grandmaster Choi constantly had a Korean news radio station playing in his office that was easily heard in the dojang.

I demonstrated the form, Sorim Kwon (Shaolin/Xiaolin Quan/Ch'uan) for Grandmaster Choi and he immediately asked me if I had trained with "Riverside" (his nickname for Grandmaster Na). I told him yes and he laughed and said, "I thought I was the only one teaching that form!"

After a little more laughter, we went back to training and he never asked me anymore about it nor discussed his relationship with Grandmaster Na. One of Grandmaster Choi's higher-ranking students had mentioned to me that Grandmaster Na trained with Grandmaster Choi in Korea, and that Grandmaster Na had even visited this Koreatown school that I was now training in.

I continued training at this school consistently, month after month and I was taken aside and given special training, both by Grandmaster Choi and by his senior-ranking instructors, since I flew so far to get there each month.

I had to relearn many of the basics that Grandmaster Young Pyo Choi had taught me during my previous 20 years with him, but it was fairly easy to do, since the modifications I had to make were only minor. Anyone who has ever transferred from one martial arts school to another (in the same art) will understand this.

After several months had passed, I got a phone call back at my school in Indy.

It was Grandmaster Na.

He told me that he would like to train me. He told me that my dedication and desire to learn the true art was something

Chapter 1. MY STORY

that very few students had.

I wasn't sure what his true intentions were, and I was a little hesitant with him. I mentioned that I was training with his teacher and I asked him why I should want to train with him when I had *his* teacher to learn from. I later learned that Grandmaster Choi Byong Yil was only one of 3 teachers that Grandmaster Na learned from in Korea.

He understood my trepidation, but asked me a very simple question that made me immediately change my mind about him. He asked me if I was learning all of the self-defense applications to each of the movements in the forms. I stopped and thought, "No."

Now, Grandmaster Choi did do a lot of one-on-one teaching with me, but he was mainly correcting my techniques and teaching me the movements. To his credit, he did teach me a few of the self-defense applications, but very few.

Funny enough, my first teacher (Grandmaster Young Pyo Choi) did not share many of the self-defense applications, either. In fact, Grandmaster Choi told me that the Kung Fu techniques wouldn't work in self-defense (which always made me wonder why he was teaching the art at all then) and that Tae Kwon Do techniques were much better for self-defense. He mainly taught us the forms and some drills that we did in each class. He modified all of his Tae Kwon Do self-defense requirements and then added Praying Mantis-style grabs to them, (in place of knife-hand blocks), to distinguish the *Kung Fu* self-defense techniques from the *Tae Kwon Do* techniques (and probably to simplify things in his school so that he wouldn't have to keep track of so many different self defense technique requirements).

Neither Grandmaster Young Pyo Choi nor Grandmaster

Byong Yil Choi worked too often with me to show me how to use the techniques from the forms in a self-defense situation, with the exception of a small handful of techniques that he showed me during our training together, and a few that Grandmaster Young Pyo Choi shared with me on ocassion, when I asked.

After thinking about Grandmaster Na's question for a moment, I humbly accepted his proposal and began adding an extra day to my trips to Los Angeles. For 4-5 days I trained with Grandmaster Na at his school in Riverside during the day (usually 6 to 8 hours) and I would then drive to Los Angeles to train with Grandmaster Choi at his Koreatown school in Los Angeles in the evenings. Sadly, Grandmaster Choi passed away in 2007.

Grandmaster Hi Seup Na, Grandmaster Byong Yil Choi and James Theros at a Korean Restaurant in 2007

Chapter 1. MY STORY

If Grandmaster Na hadn't made that phone call, I shudder to think what I would have missed out on after Grandmaster Choi passed away.

At first, Grandmaster Na was very strict with me. He never allowed me to film any of the training or his performances of the material, and was a bit reluctant to share any of the historical or background questions that I frequently asked him.

Then, one day he called me and told me that it would be alright for me to bring my camera out next time, to film the training and to capture a performance of him on video so I could bring it home to continue working on it.

I was patient and I showed him my sincerity and dedication, and he learned that I was a serious student of the art, so he allowed me those privileges, which I have never taken for granted.

After he saw some of the finished projects that I had created, he asked me to help him create some DVD's so that the art wouldn't die with him.

I began filming our entire training sessions at his school and turned them into DVD's that he could use for his school; and I got to have the footage to help with my own training.

Since that time I have trained consistently with Grandmaster Na and have conducted several interviews with him on a variety of things. The information he has shared with me is certainly a large part of the reason I was able to write my first book, and has also allowed me to have the confidence to write this book, at his urging.

Grandmaster Na is a very quiet, private man of very few words. His physical build is like that of a Korean tank. The power he is able to generate with such a small frame is remarkable and I've seen him make many men come to tears when he demonstrated self-defense techniques on the much larger opponents. His knowledge is vast and he was very fortunate to get his training during a period in time when people were less litigious about getting injured in training. He shared many stories with me about how rigorous his training was and how it made him strong.

He has a strong grasp on the internal aspects of the art as well; which is something that few of my teachers were able to teach me about.

I have traveled all around the world and have met many great masters and Grandmasters and I have yet to meet one of them with Grandmaster Na's depth of knowledge and understanding of the Chinese arts.

Grandmaster Na has never been a competitor. He has never stepped onto a tournament floor. His training has all been geared towards self-defense and realistic use of the techniques used in the forms; and conditioning his body for fighting. I've never met anyone with stronger forearms than his. He can use his forearms, during 3-star conditioning training, to strike his partner so hard that his partner usually cries "uncle!" I've personally witnessed this on more than one occasion, and felt his power myself.

His forms may not be what one would consider *pretty* because he never trained for competition, but his power and ability to inflict pain are unmistakable. His depth of knowledge about how the techniques work in real fighting is something that, until I was fortunate enough to meet him and become his personal student, far too few students ever learn.

He once told me that he doesn't openly share much of this information with any of his other students.

Prior to training with Grandmaster Na, I was left to try and *guess* as to how to use the techniques from our forms in real self-defense or to be made to believe that 90% of the techniques were "blocks" when, in fact, they are strikes. While deciphering an application from a Tae Kwon Do or Tang Soo Do form can be fairly straight forward and evident, it's much more difficult in the Chinese martial arts to understand the self-defense applications, unless one is personally shown.

I can't begin to tell you how this impacted my training in Tae Kwon Do and Tang Soo Do, and I have learned much about the art of Hapkido from the study of these forms as well. Few Korean masters teach the correlation between the art of Hapkido and the Chinese techniques from the art of Chin'Na (the art of seizing and controlling), which are prevalent in the forms of Korean Kung Fu, and many Praying Mantis systems as well.

I have interviewed Grandmaster Na several times about the art included in this book and I have hours and hours and hours of video footage of my training with him. I have had him out to my school on multiple occasions as well. When he comes to Indiana, he lives at my home for 2 weeks and we wake up at dawn and begin training (7-days-per-week from sun-up until my evening classes begin). During these training sessions he has opened up and shared things that none of my other teachers were willing to; or could it possibly have been that my other masters didn't know these things to begin with?

I'm not certain either way, but I do know how fortunate I was to have met this wonderful man and true master of this art.

It has been my personal mission since 1998 to bring it to the public. I've invested thousands of dollars in airfare and in tuition and training fees to learn this material, and I had to jump through a lot of hoops to gain access to this information.

Gaining access to this information was very similar to the way that youngsters in China would reportedly sit on the steps at the Shaolin temple for days (or months) on end, until they either gave up trying to become monks, or were finally accepted into the temple.

My story might be considered a modern-day equivalent of that. I didn't give up; I stayed persistent in my quest, and I was fortunate enough to be accepted.

I took the time to tell my story here to give the reader a better understanding of who I am, how I got involved in the martial arts, and how I found the art of Korean Kung Fu and began studying; which should give the reader a sense of confidence in what you will discover by reading this book.

Chapter Two

Gong Bu/Kung Fu
(공부)功夫

Also spelled Gong Fu/Gung Fu, the term Kung Fu can be translated as "the discipline" or "skill through training."

It can apply to literally anything. One who plays tennis well, for instance, can have Kung Fu in tennis. The term Kung Fu, for martial arts however, was not used until the 20th century.

A more accurate term for what most people think of when they hear the term Kung Fu is the term "Wu Shu" which means "War Art."

These days, however, there has been a movement towards performance-style Kung Fu, where gymnastic and balletic movements have been added into the performance to enhance its beauty.

This is what is being portrayed in most fight scenes in the movies currently and is what is known as "Modern" or "Contemporary" Wushu and, thus, when the term Wushu is mentioned, is what most Martial Artists think of.

Kung Fu is generally thought of as the more traditional way of practicing, with more emphasis on self-defense, personal and spiritual development than on performance for audiences.

Kung Fu is generally broken up into 4 categories; 2 primary categories and 2 sub-categories. The first category is northern/southern and the 2nd sub-category is hard/soft or internal/external.

Generally speaking, most Northern styles feature more kicking (and higher kicking), along with long-range striking, whereas the Southern styles feature strong footwork and shorter-range hand techniques.

An example of a very popular Northern Style would be Long Fist Kung Fu, which uses long-range strikes and many kicks above the waist; whereas a popular Southern Style, such as Hung Gar, uses many short-range strikes and kicks *below* the waist.

An external style is mainly concerned with the development of hard, external power; primarily derived from the body and muscles, with a smaller emphasis on internal energy development until the later stages in the training.

An example of a hard/external style would be Long Fist Kung Fu. Tae Kwon Do and Karate are also considered hard/external styles.

Soft/Internal styles are just the opposite of hard/external styles, where the main focus is on the development of the practitioner's Ki energy flow *first*.

Later in the training there is more emphasis on developing the external power. The internal systems are considered higher arts and take much longer to develop the skills used in them.

There are many systems of Internal Kung Fu but the 3 most common are Tai Chi Chuan, Bagua and Xing Yi. The arts of Aikido and Hapkido are also considered soft/internal arts, although the art of Hapkido has a better balance between internal and external than does Aikido.

A good majority of Kung Fu schools teach at least one hard/external style and at least one soft/internal style to achieve a good balance in training.

Chapter 2. KUNG FU

Ki Gong (Qi gong, in Chinese) training is also very common in the majority of Kung Fu schools.

It is generally believed that Kung Fu was originally brought to the famous Shaolin Temple in the year 500A.D. by a traveling Indian Monk named Bodhidharma.

Originally, Bodhidharma came to teach the monks meditation and spiritual development but he realized that the monks were physically weak due to the long periods of sitting still.

Thus he taught them Qi Gong exercises and other movements to strengthen their bodies.

The monks began to adapt these movements into what is now known as *Kung Fu*, which enabled the monks to protect the temple and themselves from the many thieves and bandits that would attack them during their trips into town for needed supplies.

From this original training came many different systems of fighting that eventually branched out into many different Shaolin systems that are in existence today.

One of these styles came by way of a few Shaolin monks who fled the Shaolin temples around the turn of the 20th century (1899-1900), when the Chinese government burned the temples in an effort to break up the rebellions caused by Shaolin.

During this time, the monks were considered fugitives by the Chinese government. In order to save themselves from death, many of the monks fled to other countries for refuge.

Once settled in their new countries some of the monks befriended local Martial Arts Masters and began sharing their knowledge.

Chapter Three

Korean Kung Fu (Sip Pal Gi)
(십팔기)十八技

One such system came to Korea around this time, but was kept underground and only taught to Chinese people living in Korea. However, around 1927, some of the Chinese masters began to open their teachings to Korean masters, due to the need to make money to pay their bills; and the art began to spread throughout South Korea.

This particular system of Kung Fu is very rare and is only taught by a handful of schools around the United States.

The system is a blend of Northern Shaolin Long Fist and Northern Praying Mantis Kung Fu.

This particular system of Kung Fu goes by many names, the most common name used is Sip Pal Gi (십 팔 기) – pronounced SHIP PAHL GEE- as in the word, "geese".

This system also goes by the name Original Northern Shaolin Kung Fu.

The name comes from the fact that this particular system was introduced to the Koreans by the Chinese monks who fled the Shaolin Temple (more on this later).

The system that was shared with the Koreans was the actual original system, which was very basic in nature, as compared to the more modern version of Kung Fu currently being taught at the Shaolin Temple in China.

The more modern style being taught at Shaolin is what is known as *Modern* Wushu.

These basic techniques have been refined and additional intricacies have been added to them over the years.

Think of a computer of today versus one of the original models back in the late 1970's.

What are the differences between the two?

The original computer screen was very big and bulky, and had only one color to display the print on the screen (usually green).

Compare that with the computers of the mid 1980's, when colors were introduced and the DOS system was created.

Now, compare the DOS system with the current version of Microsoft Windows or the latest Apple operating system and you begin to get the idea of how the "original" compares with the more modern.

In Sip Pal Gi, this is also the case.

In fact, this particular system is taught all throughout South Korea and in a handful of schools across the United States as well as in many other countries, including as far away as Greece.

Many of these schools, prior to my introducing them to one another, were unaware of each other's existence and wondered why they were unable to find other similar systems to their own, either at competitions or in books or on video.

Fortunately, the internet opened up discussions on the subject and allowed the geographical boundaries that previously existed to be widened, if not completely eradicated.

In 1998 I began searching for the missing clues to the puzzle and hit many proverbial walls and dead-ends. Fortunately, I did not give up on my quest and continued to investigate until I was able to uncover the information contained in this book.

Chapter 3. KOREAN KUNG FU

So, the term "Korean Kung Fu" is both correct *and* incorrect. It all depends on how you look at it.

Since the system is a Chinese art and came from China it can certainly be called Chinese Kung Fu.

However, since this particular style is taught predominantly by Korean masters, both in Korea *and* outside of Korea, it can also be thought of as a Korean *style* of a Chinese Martial Art.

It's also interesting to note that this particular style is the original system that helped to bridge the gap between the Chinese martial arts, the Korean martial arts and the Japanese martial arts.

If one were to look at a *Modern Wushu* form and then compare the techniques and the flow of the forms to a standard Tae Kwon Do form (particularly an older traditional one, prior to the modernized forms created by General Choi Hong Hi in the 1950's or the WTF forms created in the 1960's) one would find little resemblance, although there would still be *some* resemblance.

Now, when observing one of the traditional Sip Pal Gi Kung Fu forms it's very easy to see the similarities between modern Wushu, Tang Soo Do forms and traditional Kung Fu.

It is the opinion of the author that this Original Shaolin Kung Fu system was what was used by Grandmaster Hwang Kee (founder of Tang Soo Do/Soo Bahk Do) to create The Chil Sung and Yuk Ro forms of Tang Soo Do.

In Sip Pal Gi there are a standard set of core forms, just as there are in any other traditional Kung Fu system.

Something to note about Sip Pal Gi is that the system is *eclectic*, in that some systems lean more towards traditional

Long Fist Kung Fu, while other systems favor more traditional Northern Praying Mantis essence.

The interesting thing to note though, is that both types of schools teach the same core forms, (and the forms are easily recognizable by each school) and the forms look nearly the same, but some of the movements have more more of a Long Fist flavor vs. praying mantis, and vice versa.

Sip Pal Gi also contains many of the same standard 2-man drills and weapons forms found in other systems of Kung Fu, particularly those found in other long fist or praying mantis styles.

There is a specific long staff form and a specific broad sword form that are indigenous to Sip Pal Gi that I have not found outside the system; giving further evidence of an actual system that was passed down through the generations.

Although there are several varieties of forms that are not included in every Sip Pal Gi system (due to some of the eclectic influences from the arts of long fist, praying mantis, and even Bagua) there are a set of **core forms** that are generally found in each different Sip Pal Gi system.

I have been fortunate to make friends with many of the masters who teach this system and I've seen various structures to their curriculums, however, there are some elements of the curriculums that are congruent at each school I have visited or contacted.

The other forms outside of these core forms vary from school to school.

Here is a list of the most *common* core forms:

Chapter 3. KOREAN KUNG FU

Korean Name	Chinese Name	Korean	Chinese	English
So Chu Kwon	Xiao Zuo Quan	소축권	小縮拳	Small Reducing Fist
A Ga Kwon	Yue Jia Quan	악가권	岳家拳	Yue Family Fist
Mei Hwa kwon	Mei Hua Quan	매화권	梅花拳	Plum Blossom Fist
Kum Gang Kwon	Jin Gang Quan	금강권	金车拳	Golden Fist
Kerro Kwon	Kai Lu Quan	계로권	開路拳	Open Road Fist
Huk Ho Kwon	Hei Hu Quan	흑호권	黑虎拳	Black Tiger Fist
So Ho Yun kwon	Xiao Hu Yan Quan	소호연권	小虎燕拳	Small Flying Tiger Fist
O Ho Kwon	Wu Hu Quan	오호권	五虎拳	Five Tigers Fist

Additionally, there are two very common forms found in many Sip Pal Gi Systems that are standard praying mantis forms.

Korean Name	Chinese Name	Korean	Chinese	English
Dae Bon Go Kwon	Da Fan Che Quan	대번거권	大翻车拳	Big Carriage Wheel Fist
So Bon Go Kwon	Xiao Fan Che Quan	소번거권	小翻车拳	Small Carriage Wheel Fist

Korean systems sometimes call these forms by the names Da Ban Che Kwon and So Ban Che Kwon as well.

The most noted living Grandmaster responsible for the perpetuation of Korean Kung Fu in the 20th century is a Chinese master who moved to Korea in the early 1900's and has lived in Soeul, Korea most of his life. His name is Grandmaster Lee Duk Kang (Lee De Jiang, Chinese, 李德江).

At the time of this writing, Grandmaster Lee is still actively teaching this art in Seoul, Korea.

He has had many students who have directly, and indirectly,

trained with him that have continued his teachings all around the world.

Interestingly, Grandmaster Lee has lived in Korea since he was 18 years old but does not know how to read the Korean language, but is able to *speak* it fluently (in his own words.)

I had the privilege of meeting him in the summer of 2008 at his school in Seoul. I spent 2 days interviewing him and found him to be extremely interesting and entertaining.

Without exception, every Korean Kung Fu master I have met pays homage to him and speaks about him as one of the pioneers of the art.

James Theros with Grandmaster Lee Duk Kang, 2008

Chapter 3. KOREAN KUNG FU

There are literally hundreds of systems of Kung Fu in existence. It would be impossible for a human being to learn all there is to know about Kung Fu in his/her lifetime.

Weapons' training also plays a large part in many systems of Kung Fu. There are 18 traditional weapons (and many others outside the 18 traditional ones).

In order to learn the full array of weapons a practitioner must master the 4 core weapons (Long Staff, Broad Sword, Straight Sword and Spear).

Weapons training is also very common in the art of Sip Pal Gi. The vast majority of schools teach a full array of different weapons in their system; some schools teach all 18 of the traditional Chinese weapons but many teach the four core weapons and focus less on weapons outside of these four.

Many Sip Pal Gi schools teach a standard long staff form, known as Pal Dan Kum Bong 8단금봉 (Ba Duan Jin Gun, in Chinese), which means "8 Movements (or levels) of the Golden Staff."

The other weapon form found in most Sip Pal Gi schools is a standard broad sword form that goes by the name "O Ken Yang Do. (5 Schools/Harmonies Broad Sword)"

There has been a lot of controversy about the name of this form, and whether or not it is being correctly spelled and pronounced.

Grandmaster Lee Duk Kang mentioned that this form is called "O Ho Kuen Yan Do", which is a blend of Korean AND Chinese terms.

O in Korean means "five" (Wu, in Mandarin).

Ho, in Korean means "Tiger" (Hu, in Mandarin).

Kuen is actually a Cantonese word that means "fist." In

Mandarin the same word is Chuan; and in Korean, the word is Kwon. (See reference chart in chapter 26)

So, it is also possible that this particular broad sword form could be called "5 Tigers Fist Broad Sword," which certainly fits in with the rest of the system, since there are empty hand forms with the word "Tiger" in them.

It is also interesting to note that the opening movements of this broad sword form are exactly the same as the opening movements in the empty-hand form *So Ho Yun Kwon*, which translates as "Little Flying Tiger Fist."

Additionally, there is Huk Ho Kwon (Black Tiger Fist) and (drum roll please.....) O Ho Kwon (Five Tigers Fist).

So, it is certainly possible and feasible that this broadsword form is related to this system, and the most noted masters all teach this form. Many of them, sadly, just never did their homework to find out the historical information while they were learning their art.

From all my research to date it is my opinion, and educated guess, that, the words used to describe this broad sword form were interchanged so many times that it literally got "lost in translation."

Korean masters are notorious for blending Chinese, Japanese and Korean terms in their classrooms, so this should come as no surprise to a Korean martial arts practitioner.

Unfortunately, not all students care enough about the art that they study to ask the right questions and learn the history and translation of the forms found in their system (including those who go on to become Masters and Grandmasters!)

When this happens, important things end up being omitted or lost.

From my experience, when you ask a question about the lineage or history of a form in your system and the master is unable to give an answer, the master hides his/her ignorance by making the student feel that he should never ask questions; letting themselves off the hook of having to *answer* the question.

This was a major factor in fueling my quest for knowledge about the martial arts in general and, in particular, Sip Pal Gi.

Chapter Four

A Brief History of Korean Kung Fu

Firstly, Korean Kung Fu is actually a bit of a misnomer; Korean Kung Fu is basically, traditional Northern Shaolin Long Fist Kung Fu blended with Northern Praying Mantis Kung Fu and was taught to some Korean masters when many of the Chinese fled China during the boxer rebellion in the late 1800's and early 1900's. When the Shaolin temples were burned by the Chinese government, many of the monks had to flee, or face execution. Looking here at this map it is easy to see that Korea would have been one of the places that the Chinese would seek refuge in.

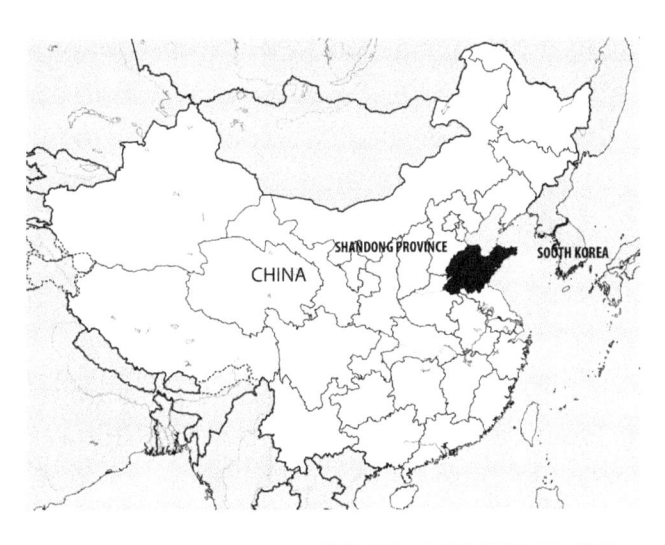

Map of Asia showing the relationship of Korea to China. The Shandong Peninsula (darkened) is a straight shot across from Incheon, South Korea

When World War II broke out, and the Japanese took control of Korea, the Koreans were forbidden to practice anything *Korean*, and much of the arts that were learned at that time (including non-martial arts that were considered "Korean") were banned. This undoubtedly suppressed the teaching and transferring of their arts from person to person.

The Korean culture had been all but obliterated by the Japanese, who sought to turn the Koreans into Japanese citizens. However, when World War II came to an end, the Koreans were freed from Japanese rule and began to rapidly try and put their culture back together.

Keep in mind that indigenous Korean people live a different lifestyle than Chinese people do. They are brought up differently and they have their own unique identity. This identity has obviously been *influenced* by both China and Japan, however, since Korea is literally in between the two countries, and, as such, it is a given that both China and Japan would have an influence on all things Korean; just as in America we have been influenced by those who have come to our country from other lands by way of the African-Americans who were brought here from Africa and were "Americanized."

So, while we Americans have picked up habits and vernacular from these countries, we have made everything very "American."

Even the food in *American* Chinese restaurants is quite unique to America. If you were to travel to China you would notice that their Chinese food is a bit different from what we are served in Chinese restaurants here in America.

So, what does that have to do with the martial arts and Korean Kung Fu? Everything.

Chapter 4. A BRIEF HISTORY OF KOREAN KUNG FU

While the art is a Chinese art, the Koreans adapted and modified some of the essence of the original system; not because they *meant* to, but, because they are from a different culture; it just *happened*.

When watching a Korean master performing Kung Fu and then comparing him to his Chinese counterpart (even though they may be performing the very same form) it is fairly easy to spot the Korean practitioner by their more rigid way of moving.

Koreans, by nature, are a bit more rigid than Chinese in nearly all ways---more about that from Grandmaster Na in his interview later in this book. So, Korean Kung Fu has actually become a "style," for lack of a better term, because of the way that the Korean culture has influenced the essence of this Chinese art.

Additionally, as you will learn from the interviews contained in this book, the Chinese who taught the Koreans purposely taught the Koreans differently than they taught their Chinese students; which is a common practice in the marital arts.

It may be difficult for our younger generation to comprehend this, since today we have so much access to information and we can quickly sift through the generous amount of available information at our fingertips. Today, we have the internet and Google; YouTube; Facebook; the nearly unlimited books through places like Amazon.com and Kindle; and there are countless websites with information on virtually everything we could ever hope to learn.

Before we had all this access though, it was fairly easy to keep information secret and for people to purposely give misinformation to keep proprietary information from getting out. The martial arts mindset was quite different at that time, and people guarded their information much more closely than today.

Even to this day, at most Chinese martial arts competitions, many of the competitors frown on having their forms recorded on video by anyone other than someone from their own system.

So, even though I call my art *Korean* Kung Fu, I have had enough training with Chinese masters to be able to see where many of the adaptations to techniques were, and to understand the *way* that my Korean masters move in comparison to my Chinese masters. I've been able to draw the parallels between the arts in a way that many of my Korean masters may not have not been interested in doing.

As an example, when I first began competing with the forms I learned from Grandmaster Young Pyo Choi back in the mid-90's I seldom did well in pure *Kung Fu* competitions, because my performances looked a bit too rigid and I couldn't figure out why I would do so well with the very same form when I competed at a Tang Soo Do or Tae Kwon Do tournament. It took several years for me to place in the top 3 at any of the Chinese-based tournaments, because I didn't fully understand *Chinese movement;* because I had been taught by a *Korean* master.

While Grandmaster Young Pyo Choi's movements are still very beautiful and graceful (much more so than any of his Korean peers that I've witnessed) there is still a *Korean* look to his movements, and this is particularly obvious when observing his Tai Chi form.

Chapter 4. A BRIEF HISTORY OF KOREAN KUNG FU

After I trained with my Wushu teacher, Master Kenny Perez, and with *his* teachers (the famed Coach Wu Bin, who also taught Jet Li and Donnie Yen), I began to understand some of the subtleties, which I then added into my performances, and I began placing at both Korean and Chinese competitions.

I devoured every book and DVD on Northern Long Fist and Praying Mantis that I could find, since those two arts comprised the Kung Fu system that I was learning.

I wanted to see where the differences were in what I was learning and what the Chinese masters did. I was able to begin modifying my motions and techniques, *ever so slightly*, so that I was able to easily *blend in* with all of the other traditional Chinese competitors; and I began to succeed at placing ahead of many of the Chinese competitors at these tournaments in the traditional divisions.

After 20 years of competing, in 2002 I retired from competition to focus more on my own training, and to spend time building my school so that I could run it full time. In 2012, I returned to competition and traveled all across the United States, competing in as many types of tournaments as possible. I competed in 10 tournaments across the country. I made it my goal to compete in tournaments in all 4 quadrants of the United States (north, south, east and west); from Los Angeles to New York and from Texas to Michigan and a few in the mid-west). I competed in Tang Soo Do-only competitions, Tae Kwon Do-only competitions, open competitions (including The Battle of Atlanta), and Kung Fu-only tournaments, (including Sifu Jimmy Wong's "Legends of Kung Fu Championships" in Houston, Texas) and I took first place over several other Chinese competitors in both forms and weapons, using the form So Ho Yun and two different long staff forms (one was a basic Wushu long staff form that I learned from Master Kenny Perez and the other was Pal Dan Kum Bong, which is a standard long staff form of Korean Kung Fu).

Nobody who watched me or competed with me questioned the authenticity of my skills. In fact, I received numerous compliments from many of the Chinese masters and competitors.

I mention this not to be boastful, but to show that this Korean style of Kung Fu is valid and has merit. Chinese martial arts, like most other arts, are constantly evolving.

The way that the Chinese perform today is vastly different than the way they performed 30 years ago. Wushu played a large part of the evolution of the Chinese martial arts and has influenced the traditional arts much the same way that modern-day Tae Kwon Do has influenced the majority of other Korean martial arts.

James Theros with Sifu Jimmy Wong at the Legends of Kung Fu Tournament in Houston, Texas, 2012.

James Theros with Grandmaster C.S. Kim, Pittsburgh 2012

Chapter 4. A BRIEF HISTORY OF KOREAN KUNG FU

It's actually becoming difficult to tell one art from another, with the exception of the uniforms worn. This is obviously due to the increased access to information these days; and the UFC has certainly shown martial artists that there is something to be learned from just about any art. As a result, many traditional martial arts systems have begun to include grappling skills into their original art (even if just the basics), which will undoubtedly have a huge impact on what a Tae Kwon Do, Tang Soo Do, Karate, Kung Fu, or Hapkido art will look like in the next 20 years.

Therefore, the Korean Kung Fu masters have something quite unique when you think about it. They have basically preserved a traditional art that was passed on to them by the Chinese; while the Chinese masters have gone on to make innovations and changes to their own martial arts. So, in essence, the Korean Kung Fu system (Sip Pal Gi) is like a *time-capsule*, in that it is still being practiced much the same way as it had been taught many, many years ago, unlike other arts that have evolved over the past 40 years.

This generation, though, may be the last generation to have experience in this system as it exists today, because many of the schools that teach this system, both here in the United States and in other countries, including Korea, have begun to adapt and modify their training to include some of the more modern Wushu techniques in their system.

I like to think about it this way; People had a certain way that they dressed and spoke, back in the 1940's. The cars that they drove, while very functional at the time and generally very large, in contrast to today's automobile, would look and sound a bit strange in today's world.

Imagine seeing a person, dressed like a 1940's businessman with a 1940's hairstyle, standing in line at a sore or seated at a table next to you at restaurant. Imagine seeing the type of mustaches worn back in those days, today. Imagine speaking with someone who used 1940's language. It would look and sound odd to us.

The point is, people adapt and modify to be *up with the times*. Even boxing is very different today than it was in the early 1900's. The way that they held their hands, and the amount of movement and footwork were vastly different from what today's boxers look like in the ring. Same goes for basketball, race-car driving (and their cars), etc....

So, it's important to modify and update our martial arts as well. This is why Korean Kung Fu, as it is today, will likely look more like what the Chinese practitioners are currently doing, in the near future.

It is important that martial arts teachers and students learn about their arts by studying the past. Studying the past, including the mindsets of cultures who came before us, is very revealing and can greatly enhance our knowledge and confidence, and can greatly improve one's confidence as a practitioner.

A person who helped to build computers in the 1970's has a distinct advantage over someone who recently learned how to build one of today's computers (as long as they have also kept up with modern technology), if for no other reason than because the former has knowledge and experience that the latter has not had, and that creates a different paradigm for the former and gives that person the ability to understand the evolution of technology, which creates a more stable platform for that older technician when things go wrong.

I believe it is no different for a martial artist, and this is part of where *wisdom* comes from in the martial arts.

Consequently, part of my mission in my research is to insure that there is some evidence of the traditional system of Kung Fu that was brought from Northern China to South Korea and will continue to be taught, so that future generations may be able to come back and revisit some of this important historical information and to help further their knowledge about the ancestry of the art that they are practicing.

The Pioneers of Korean Kung Fu

LIM POOM JANG

Lim Poom Jang/Lin Ping Jiang (1910-1982)
Praying Mantis Kung Fu Pioneer in Korea

Grandmaster Lim Poom Jang was born in 1910. According to Korean oral tradition, he was born in Manchuria. His master was Ji Chung Ting.

Later, Lim Poom Jang emigrated from the Shan Dong Province to Korea in the late 40's or early 50's. He first taught in Chuncheon. Then he was invited to Seoul by the Chinese Resident's Association to teach, and he accepted a post as physical education teacher for the Chinese Primary school in Myongdong. A school was set up, within the embassy initially, and this was the beginning of praying mantis instruction in Seoul.

NO SU JUN

No Su Jun/ Liu Xiu Tian (1894-1978)
Bagua Zhang Kung Fu Pioneer in Korea

Grandmaster No Su Jun was born in Ching Tao China in 1894. He was known for his skill in the art of Bagua and helped to spread the art throughout South Korea around the same time as Grandmasters Lim Poom Jang and Lee Duk Kang. He is responsible for adding Bagua into many of the Korean Kung Fu systems and those masters who teach Bagua in their curriculum owe their lineage to him. One of his most noted students is Park Bok Nam, who teaches a system called Sip Pal Ki that is more of a self-created art. Grandmaster Park declined an interview for this book.

LEE DUK KANG

Lee Duk Kang/Li De Jiang (1931-)
Long Fist Kung Fu Pioneer in Korea

Grandmaster Lee Duk Kang was born in Yen Tai, Shandong Province China in 1931. He is also called Yi Po (sometimes Pyo) Hyung as well. Grandmaster Lee is responsible for helping to spread Northern Long Fist throughout South Korea and many of today's teachers have lineage that connects back to him.

Chapter 4. A BRIEF HISTORY OF KOREAN KUNG FU

HWANG JU HWAN

Hwang Ju Hwan (黃柱煥, 황주환)
Pioneer of Korean Kung Fu

Grandmaster Hwng Ju Hwan is very famous for his Kung Fu prowess. He is known as the *Godfather of Kung Fu in Korea*. He began his training at the age of 17, in the year 1956, in Pusan, South Korea. His teachers were Master Song and Master Du (Chinese masters). He then moved to Seoul, South Korea and began studying with Lim Poom Jang, Seung Un Seung and others. He traveled frequently and trained with 35 different masters to learn Kung Fu.

KO KWANG YU

Ko Kwang Yu

I was unable to ascertain any concrete information about Grandmaster Ko Kwang Yu for this book, but he is always mentioned as one of the pioneers of the art. This was the only photo I was able to locate.

KANG KYUNG BANG
Jiang Geng Fang (1912-1994)
(No Picture Available)

Grandmaster Kang Kyung Bang was born in Shandong China. Born in 1912 he was student of Hao Heng Lu. He emigrated from Shandong, China to Korea in the 1940's. He was close friend of Lim Poom Jang. He used to live and teach in Pusan, South Korea and occasionally on Je Ju Do Island. He traveled regularly to Taiwan to train his students over there. Grandmaster Kang Kyung Bang passed away in in 1994.

Chapter Five

Myung Sang/Ming Xian
(명상)冥想

Meditation is an important part part in Kung Fu training. There are many ways of meditating and there are several purposes for meditation.

Meditation in the martial arts is used to clear the mind and prepare the student for learning by ridding oneself of all extraneous thoughts that may impede learning and progress.

Meditation should be practiced just before Kung Fu training and just after training.

Before training, the focus should be on *clearing* and *calming* the mind– similar to erasing a chalkboard before using it.

After practice, meditation is used to reflect on what was learned during the practice, or to creatively visualize one's goals in the martial arts or in life.

Meditation can be done standing, sitting or lying down. Standing meditation is often performed using the "Post" position or the "Tree-hugging" position, found in many Qigong systems.

A chair can be used as well, which helps the practitioner to maintain a very straight spine (to allow for best Qi flow) and is more comfortable than sitting on the floor, but is not practical in many martial arts schools, since there is usually a group of people involved.

Meditation can be as short as 30-60 seconds for a quick prep to learning or as long as an hour to several hours for deep reflection and enlightenment.

For longer meditation sessions a cushion is recommended to allow the practitioner to relax while maintaining a straight posture throughout the session.

Soft music can also be played in the background to further relax oneself.

For seated meditation there are generally 4 postures one may use. The first posture is the Lotus position, which is generally what people think of when they hear the word "meditation" in which the practitioner folds both legs, one on top of the other, at the ankles, knees, and thighs flat on the ground. This posture requires more flexibility.

Lotus

The next variation is the *half lotus*, in which only one of the legs is folded on top of the other, with both knees flat as possible.

Half Lotus

Chapter 5. MEDITATION

The third posture, usually used by those with less flexibility is the standard cross-legged seated position, in which the practitioner folds the legs under the other and tries to keep both knees as close to the floor as possible.

Cross-Leg

The 4th posture (used a bit more by Korean & Japanese stylists) is what the Japanese call *Seiza*, which means "correct sitting" posture.

Seiza

This is done by simply sitting back against the feet with the tops of the feet flat against the floor.

The arms should be relaxed and the hands may be lightly placed in the lap with the thumbs connected (to connect Qi flow).

The tip of the tongue should touch the upper palate (either just behind the two front teeth, directly in the middle of the palate, or at the very back of the palate) to connect the meridians and allow for better Qi flow.

Breathing is best done strictly through the nose but breathing in through the nose and exhaling through the mouth is also acceptable (or an interchange between the two methods can be used).

Breathing solely through the nose eliminates dryness in the back of the throat that can occur when breathing through the mouth.

It is also more difficult to breathe through the mouth when the tongue is touched to the roof of the mouth (palate).

Thoughts should be only on one's breathing. Breathing should be deep and relaxed and should be directed at the abdomen.

The abdomen should rise with each inhalation and fall with each exhalation.

Once a state of relaxation has been achieved, one may choose to do *ratio*-breathing, which allows one to direct energy to various parts of the body.

To perform ratio breathing, inhale for a count of 7, hold the breath and circulate it for a count of 28, then exhale for a count of 14.

During meditation attempt to get in touch with your inner energy; attempt to locate the Qi flow.

Once you are able to sense your Qi, begin to circulate it through the "microcosmic orbit," which is basically the head and torso.

Chapter 5. MEDITATION

Begin by bringing your attention to your navel area. Then, direct the Qi down to the Dan Tian (Danjun) area, about 2 to 3 inches below the navel.

Then circulate it down to the perineum (the area between the sexual center and the anus). Send the energy up to the Sacrum (the triangular bone at the bottom of the spine), then up to the *Ming Men* area (The Door of Life– opposite of the navel, on the back).

Continue sending the energy up the spine to the cranial area (occiput), and then to the very top of the head (crown), and down the front of the forehead to the 3rd eye area (pineal gland).

Continue the energy down to the throat area and down to the solar plexus area and finally back to the navel. Continue sending this energy around the microcosmic orbit for as many times as you like, each time feeling the energy grow warmer and more vibrant.

When you are ready to finish, bring the energy back to the navel and circulate it clockwise (Counter-clockwise for females) 36 times. Then reverse the direction for 24 circles in the opposite direction.

This acts to seal the energy in your Dan Tian (Danjun). The Dan Tian is your lower diaphragm or *energy* center.

Meditation is also a great source of learning to cultivate inner peace, and daily meditation of no more than 10-15 minutes can make a measurable difference in your ability to cope with stress, help lower blood pressure, and reduce anxiety.

Chapter Six
Ki Gong (Chi Gong)
(기공)氣功

Qi Gong (in Chinese, Qigong, also spelled Chi Kung) Qi Gong means Training of Energy.

Ki means "energy." The energy that is referred to is the special *life-energy* inside of every living being. It is an electrical pulse that runs through the body throughout special "meridians."

These meridians are like a highway system running throughout the body, in which the energy travels to various parts of the body, bringing blood, oxygen and Ki to nourish and heal the body, or to add power or strength to a technique.

When there is a blockage of Ki flow in the body, injury or illness may occur.

These meridians are used in acupuncture and acupressure to heal, and are used in martial arts self-defense to harm.

"Gong" or Kung means "Training" or "Development."

The art of Qi Gong has short *forms* designed with specific movements, breathing, and direction of thought to help achieve improved Ki flow in the body that bring about increased energy levels, increased circulation, emotional well-being, better health and vitality and a deeper level of spiritual connection with the earth and the heavens.

There are as many Qi Gong systems in existence as there are systems of Kung Fu. All are good. All are beneficial.

A few of the Qi Gong techniques are very common in each of these systems, due to their effectiveness.

Qi Gong was part of the training of the Shaolin Monks thousands of years ago and is still practiced today in many Kung Fu schools to aid in the development of the practitioner's health & vitality, and to increase power in blocks, strikes and kicks; with the additional benefit of making the practitioner's ability to absorb strikes, with reduced chance of injury, possible.

As with Kung Fu, Qi Gong is broken into Hard Styles and Soft Styles. The differences are mainly found in the breathing and muscle work.

Hard styles of Qi Gong generally feature labored-breathing, or breathing through one's clenched teeth, while tensing certain muscles, and then relaxing.

Many styles of Karate use this type of Qi Gong, and even feature some strange sounds emitted from the throat to increase the Ki flow in the body.

Soft styles of Qi Gong generally feature relaxed breathing and stationary postures or slow, rhythmic movements (usually while standing in one place or with very few movements of the legs).

The soft styles of Qi Gong are the precursors to Tai Chi Chuan practice, which is considered to be a more advanced practice of Qi Gong.

Tai Chi Chuan is sometimes referred to as "moving meditation."

Two of the most popular sets of Qi Gong practice are: The 8-Section Brocade (Ba Duan Jin, 八段錦) and The Muscle

Tendon Change Classic (Yi Jin Jing, 易筋經).

These systems have been in use for thousands of years and continue to be practiced by many Kung Fu practitioners (and non-practitioners) around the globe.

Some systems of Qi Gong also use special healing sounds, created with the voice, to help increase Ki flow in the body.

Chapter Seven

Pal Dan Kum / Ba Duan Jin
(팔단금)八段錦

The 8-Section Brocade (also known as the 8 Pieces of Silk Brocade) is reported to be the oldest recorded exercise in Chinese history.

It is practiced in many Kung Fu schools as a warm up to more rigorous exercise since it has an effect on the central nervous system, the cardiovascular system, and the musculoskeletal system, as well as massaging of internal organs.

Many Sip Pal Gi schools use this set (called Pal Dan Kum, in Korean) in their schools, along with other breathing exercises to help their students develop stronger Ki.

Regular practice of the 8-Section Brocade form will benefit all of the internal organs (including the lung, liver, heart, spleen and pericardium—the protective layer of the heart).

The circulatory and respiratory systems will be improved; better concentration, physical and mental strength, along with strengthening the joints, sinew, muscle and the entire body.

An increased metabolism and regulation of the digestive system will also occur.

There are 8 simple exercises (and several variations of these 8 exercises) that make up the routine. The names for the 8 exercises and the benefits of each exercise are as follows:

#1- Double Hands Hold Up the Heavens

Regulates the organs and increases Qi circulation in the front of the body.

Begin with feet together, fingers intertwined (palms up). Slowly raise up onto toes (heels together) inhale and slowly lift and rotate the palms upward and gently stretch upward while inhaling. Slowly lower hands and rotate palms back to original position while exhaling slowly. Perform at least twice, or up to 8 times if time allows.

Chapter 7. THE 8-SECTION BROCADE

#2- Pushing Heaven and Earth

Regulates spleen, stomach & digestive system.

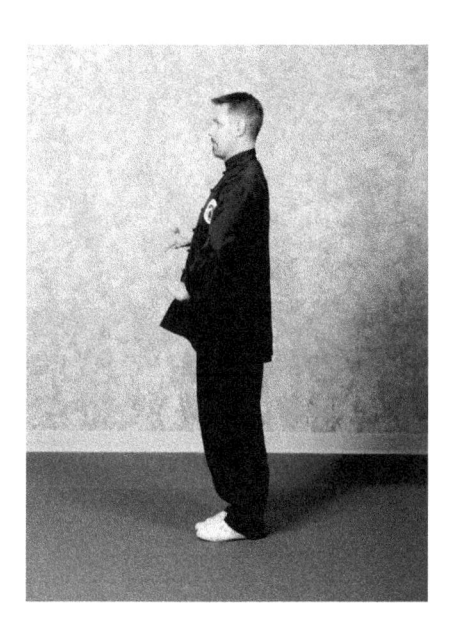

Begin with feet together, left palm facing the floor and right palm facing upward (no tension in either hand). Slowly raise up on toes (heels together) and gently push right hand upward while gently pushing left hand downward and looking back and down at your left hand. Exhale and slowly switch the positions of your hands. Be sure to keep your eyes on the hand that pushes downward.

#3– Wise Owl Gazes Backward

Alleviates mental fatigue and calms the central nervous system, cures illness caused by weakness of the five yin organs (heart, liver, spleen, lungs, kidney) and injuries from the seven emotions (happiness, anger, sorrow, joy, love, hate, and desire).

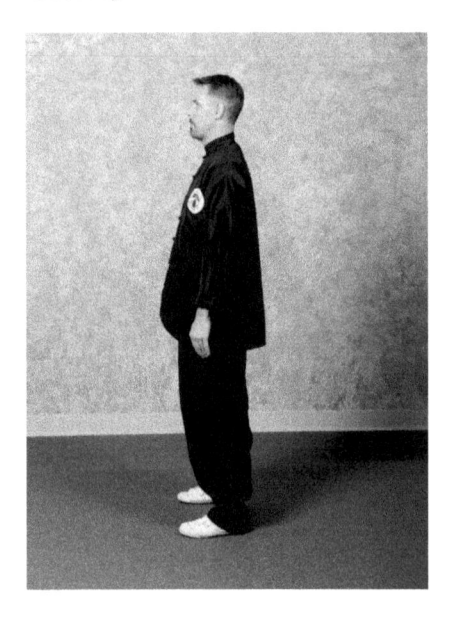

Begin with feet shoulder-width apart. Inhale deeply and then slowly exhale and turn and look over your left shoulder at your right heel. Hold for a brief moment, then inhale and slowly turn over the opposite shoulder and look at your other heel. Repeat at least twice.

Chapter 7. THE 8-SECTION BROCADE

#4- Bend the Bow
Strengthens waist and kidneys, increases metabolism.

Begin in riding horse stance (feet double shoulder-width apart), hands at your sides. Inhale and slowly rotate your upper body to the left and form a single-finger tiger claw with your left hand. Then, hook your right index finger onto your left thumb (for resistance) and exhale as you pull the hands apart with a slight tension in your muscles (known as dynamic tension). Push out your chest on the extension (the "pointing" finger can point to the left, as shown, or it can be held in a standard upright position, as in a traditional tiger claw as in the first picture). Inhale and reset your chest and hands and turn to the other side to repeat.

#5– Big Bear Turns from Side to Side

Gets rid of heartburn & loosens the leg muscles, removes abnormal nervous tension and regulates the excretory functions' process by which the waste products of the metabolism or undigested food residues are eliminated from the body by relaxing the body.

Begin in riding horse stance (feet double shoulder-width apart), hands at your sides. Inhale deeply and then slowly exhale and lean your body to the left, hands touching thighs, and slowly try to lean as far as possible while your hand moves down your shin and attempts to touch the floor next to your left foot. Inhale as you return to the beginning posture and repeat to the right side. As in each of these, do two times each side minimum, up to 8 if time permits.

#6- Screw the Fist with Fiery Eyes

Raises the flow of vitality, strengthens Qi flow and increases muscular strength, promotes development of muscles and increases physical strength and endurance. The concentrated focusing of the eyes will increase both mental and physical strength.

Begin in riding horse stance (feet double shoulder-width apart), fists chambered at your sides. Raise up onto your toes, suck in your chest and protrude your back, then slowly rotate your right fist over as you slowly punch out with a loose fist (as your fist reaches its destination, protrude your chest out and then retract it as you begin retracting your fist). Punch slowly and continuously (one hand goes out while the other hand comes back) for a count of 8-10 punches. Stare at an object straight ahead and off at a distance and put a look of intensity in your eyes throughout the exercise. Power can be put into the final-third of the punch as well to enhance one's *fajing* (explosive energy).

#7- Two Hands Hold the Feet

Strengthens kidneys and waist, extends and makes more elastic the area around the waist involving the movements of the abdomen and every tissue and organ included in it.

Begin with feet together, hands at your sides. Inhale deeply and then slowly bend forward and exhale, lowering yourself one vertebrae at a time. Gently hold onto your ankles and pull your body forwards to pull yourself lower. If possible, pull your chest all the way to your thighs. Hold for a brief moment and then slowly raise your body one vertebrae at a time. When you reach the top of the movement, gently shrug your shoulders backward once to release any tension and then repeat.

#8– Vibrate the back 7 Times

Smoothes Ki from the top of the head to the bottom of the feet, removes disease, helps both loosening and tightening of the joints, relaxes shoulder blades and shoulders.

Begin with feet shoulder-width apart. Exhale and quickly drop forward, allowing your hands to touch the floor between your feet (palms up, backs of hands touching the floor) and then inhale as you bridge your back backward and swing your hands up and back until they reach your kidneys (hands open, palms touching kidneys). Bend back as far as you can and hold for a moment of pure bliss. Then, repeat.

Chapter Eight

Tae Geuk Kwon/Tai Chi Chuan
(태극권)太極拳

Tae Geuk Kwon, known by its much more popular Chinese name, Tai Chi Chuan (also spelled Taiji Quan) is considered the most popular of all the internal martial arts.

Within the Tai Chi family there are 4 main branches, or *families* and these families are *Yang Style, Chen Style, Wu Style and Sun Style,* and there is also a lesser-known style of Tai Chi called the Hao Style (formerly known as the Wu-Yu Xiang Style).

While each of the four styles is based on the same concepts, each style has its own distinct methodology.

Chen Style Tai Chi Chuan

The Chen Style of Tai Chi looks and feels closer to actual *Kung Fu*, with lots of circular, powerful "jerky" motions and spiraling of the body to generate power. It is considered the oldest of all Tai Chi Styles and spawned all the other styles in existence today.

There is a concept called "Silk Reeling" used in this particular style of Tai Chi that is a very popular type of Qi Gong (Qigong) used in specific martial arts. Chen Style Tai Chi is the second most widely practiced style of Tai Chi in the world, next to yang Style

Yang Style Tai Chi Chuan

The Yang Style of Tai Chi Chuan is the most widely practiced of all Tai Chi systems and is generally what most people think of when they hear the words *Tai Chi*. The movements are very large and performed slowly and fluidly. It is sometimes referred to as "moving meditation."

Yang style Tai Chi takes up where Qigong leaves off, and is generally the next level of Qigong practice. Many movements of Yang Tai Chi are taken directly from Qigong movements.

Wu Style Tai Chi Chuan

The Wu Style of Tai Chi also uses the Silk Reeling exercises, used in Chen style. Wu Style Tai Chi Chuan shares some of the same principles of Yang Style Tai Chi but favors smaller movements over the Yang Style's larger ones. The feet are usually kept closer together while performing as well. One of the more significant features of the Wu Style is that more grappling and joint-locking techniques are taught in the beginner stages.

Sun Style Tai Chi Chuan

The Sun Style Tai Chi is known for its smooth, flowing movements, which is completely devoid of the more vigorous crouching, leaping and power of some of the other styles. The footwork of Sun Style is also a bit different than the other styles, in that when one foot advances or retreats the other follows.

Sun Style also uses an open palm throughout the performance of its forms, and uses small circular movements with the hand, similar to Wu Style.

Hao Style Tai Chi Chuan

The lesser known Hao Style is a very distinctive style featuring small, subtle movements; focused on balance, sensitivity and internal Qi development. It is a rare style today, and not many schools exist, outside of China, that teach this particular style.

Tae Geuk Kwon (Tai Chi Chuan) literally means "Grand Ultimate Fist," and is based on the principles of *Yin* and *Yang*.

Tai Chi Chuan, although it looks more like a dance, is based on sound Martial Arts principles of self-defense. Kung Fu practitioners who also study Tai Chi develop a better understanding for principles of movement used in their external styles of Kung Fu and also develop better balance and flexibility as a result of the practice.

Tai Chi can also be practiced strictly for health benefits and it is very common to see large groups of senior citizens practicing Tai Chi in parks around the world.

Nearly all Sip Pal Gi schools incorporate Tae Geuk Kwon (the Korean way of saying Tai Chi Chuan) into their training.

Some schools teach this at the beginning levels, and some schools reserve this training for students after black sash, to help balance out their *external* training with some *internal* training.

The majority of schools teach either the Yang 24-Step form and/or the 48-Combined Tai Chi form.

There are some slight differences in a few of the basics of the Korean practitioners (usually small things such as what stance the practitioner uses for a movement, such as using what's known as a "T-Stance" where a Chinese practitioner would use a "Cat Stance" and vice versa.)

Overall though, the forms are identical and indistinguishable, since they both come from the same root form (the Yang Style 108 long form).

Schools who teach this form also generally teach a recognizable Iron Fan form that is a standard Tai Chi fan form, known as the Tai Chi 52-Step Fan Form.

Combined-Style Tai Chi

There are also two Tai Chi forms in existence that were created using elements from all four of the main styles. The first, and most popular of these forms is the 48-Combined Tai Chi form.

This form was created in 1976 by three Chinese masters to help practitioners of Tai Chi progress faster and to be able to give them some experience in all four styles of Tai Chi.

The other combined form is the 42 Step Form. The biggest difference between the two is that, in the 42 Form, the 4 main styles are not equally represented, whereas in the 48-Combined form, they are.

Push Hands Practice

Push Hands practice is also a very common practice in Tai Chi. It helps practitioners develop better balance and the ability to sense an opponent's intention while using points of leverage to off-balance their opponent. It is the living embodiment of the Yin and Yang principle.

When the opponent pushes you, yield and allow him to lose his energy by non-resistance. If he pulls, you gently push and allow him to lose his balance.

When the opponent is vulnerable and off-balance, you simply apply a small amount of pressure to him and send him in the direction he is already traveling, but at a greater speed. While simplistic in nature, It takes years of practice to develop push hands skills, but once developed, your understanding of balance and power will be increased and allow you the ability to easily upset your opponent's balance in a self-defense situation.

Tai Chi Taught in Korea

The style of Tai Chi (Tae Geuk Kwon) taught in Korea is identical to those taught in China. The most two common Tai Chi systems taught in Korea are Yang and Chen and there are many excellent books about these arts available.

The Korean terms for Yang and Chen Tai Chi are as follows:
Yang= Yang Ga Sik (양가식)
Chen=Jin Sik (진 식)
Sik 식 means style.

10 Important Points of Tai Chi Practice

Focusing on the 10 important steps will allow you to excel in your Tai Chi training. If the following 10 keys are not followed, then you are not really practicing Tai Chi.

1. Relax
The most important element of proper Tai Chi practice is relaxing. This is harder than it sounds and takes lots of practice to achieve.

2. Sink
To sink means to relax completely. The entire body should be relaxed. All the energy should be focused in the "Bubbling

Well Point" (a hollow place in the middle of the sole of the foot.)

When one has reached this high level of development, the Qi will sink deeply to the Dan Tien, and one's movements will be light and graceful.

3. The chest should be held in, the back straightened, the shoulders sunk, and the elbows lowered.

The chest should be slightly concave (rather than protruding) and the back should be straightened as if against an imaginary wall. The elbows should point downwards towards the ground, rather than pointing out sideways.

4. A light energy should be preserved on the top of the head. The lowest vertebrae should be erect.

The head should feel as if it is suspended from above by a string attached to a balloon, which will make the body feel graceful and light.

Keep a light energy on the very top of the head, as if suspended from above by a string, to prevent you from collapsing.

The lowest vertebrae should be erect, which will keep the mind clear.

5. All the movements are directed by the mind. Do not use external muscular force.

Use the mind to direct the movements, which will then be graceful and light. If you use external muscular force to direct the movements, they will be heavy and uncoordinated.

"From the most flexible and yielding one will arrive at the most powerful and unyielding."

6. Upper parts and lower parts follow each other, and the whole body acts as one unit.

When the hands move, the body and legs immediately move also, so that the whole body is in unison.

7. Insubstantial and substantial must be clearly differentiated.

When practicing Tai Chi it is very important to distinguish between the insubstantial and substantial aspects.

For example, if the whole body's weight is on the right foot, the right foot is substantial and the left foot is insubstantial, and vice versa.

Doing this makes the movement of steps and turning of the body graceful and light. Otherwise the steps will be heavy and uncoordinated, and the practitioner can be thrown off balance with a slight pull and push by an opponent.

While stepping forward with the right foot, first shift the entire weight to the left foot, leaving no weight on the right foot - then the movement will be graceful and light.

8. Concentrate on the line of vision.

Your eyes must look forward at an imaginary opponent in front of you, watching him constantly to see how he might attack you.

When your body turns in one direction, your eyes must look forward in the same direction. It is incorrect to look left while your body is facing right. The head and body should be considered one unit.

9. All the movements must be connected without severance. When energy is severed, use mind-intent to reconnect it.

All the postures are to be practiced slowly, effortlessly and continuously, so that the Ki and blood can circulate through the entire body without hindrance.

During the transition from one posture to another, you must stop for just half a second. This momentary stoppage will be connected and joined to the next posture by the mind-intent.

If one goes on to another posture before the preceding one is fully completed, it will be improper and will not be "continuously moving."

10. Meditation in action

Control the movements by remaining tranquil, and direct the movements by mind-intent, rather than by external muscular force.

Then the movements will be effortless, continuous, and slow. The slower one practices (without stopping or jerking) the better.

Chapter 8. INTERNAL MARTIAL ARTS TRAINING

Yang Tai Chi 24-Step Form

The Yang 24-step Tai Chi form is the world's most popular Tai Chi form. It is also known as the Yang Short Form and is often seen in competitions, due to its relatively short pattern, when compared to other Tai Chi forms.

The 24-Step form was created around 1956 in China and was created as a shorter version of the Tai Chi Long Form or the Tai Chi 108-Step Form.

When this form is performed at the proper speed it should take the practitioner between 5 and 7 minutes to complete. In many competitions, the time limit is only 3 minutes (for a very good reason---it would literally take "all day" to finish a division if competitors were to perform the entire routine at the normal speed!)

In competition, it is acceptable to move through the form a little faster than normal, however, when practicing the form for its health benefits it is advisable to practice the form much slower and to repeat the form at least 3 to 5 times each practice session.

I am presenting a pictorial of this form for a general understanding of what the form looks like. It is important to seek out instruction from a qualified instructor of Tai Chi in order to learn the many important subtle details of Tai Chi and to learn proper movement.

Don't let the slow, simplistic motion fool you into thinking that learning Tai Chi is easy. Tai Chi is an internal martial art, and internal martial arts actually take much longer to get good at, and a lifetime to master them.

Korean Kung Fu: The Chinese Connection

76

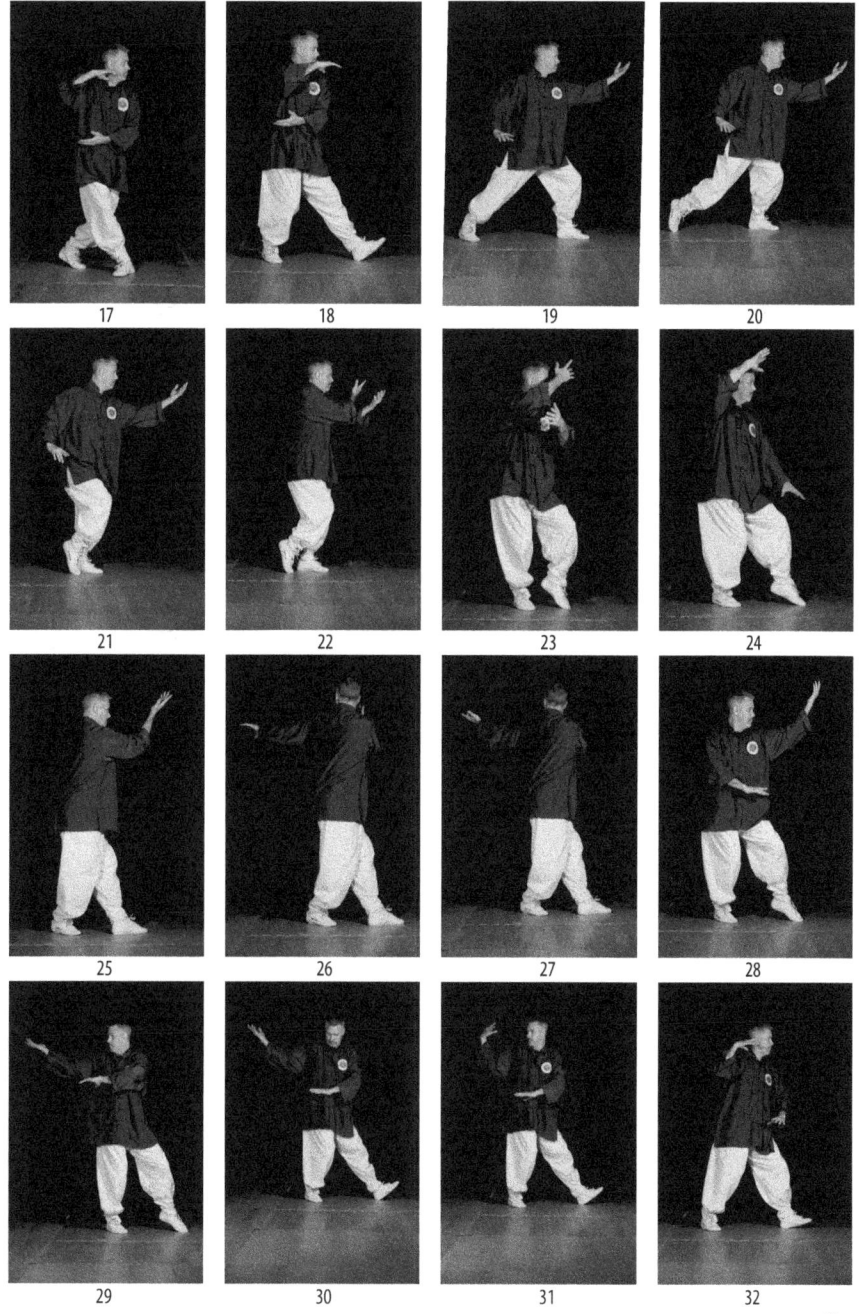

Chapter 8. INTERNAL MARTIAL ARTS TRAINING

Korean Kung Fu: The Chinese Connection

33 34 35 36

37 38 39 40

41 42 43 44

45 46 47 48

Chapter 8. INTERNAL MARTIAL ARTS TRAINING

49	50	51	52
53	54	55	56
57	58	59	60
61	62	63	64

Korean Kung Fu: The Chinese Connection

65 66 67 68
69 70 71 72
73 74 75 76
77 78 79 80

80

Chapter 8. INTERNAL MARTIAL ARTS TRAINING

81

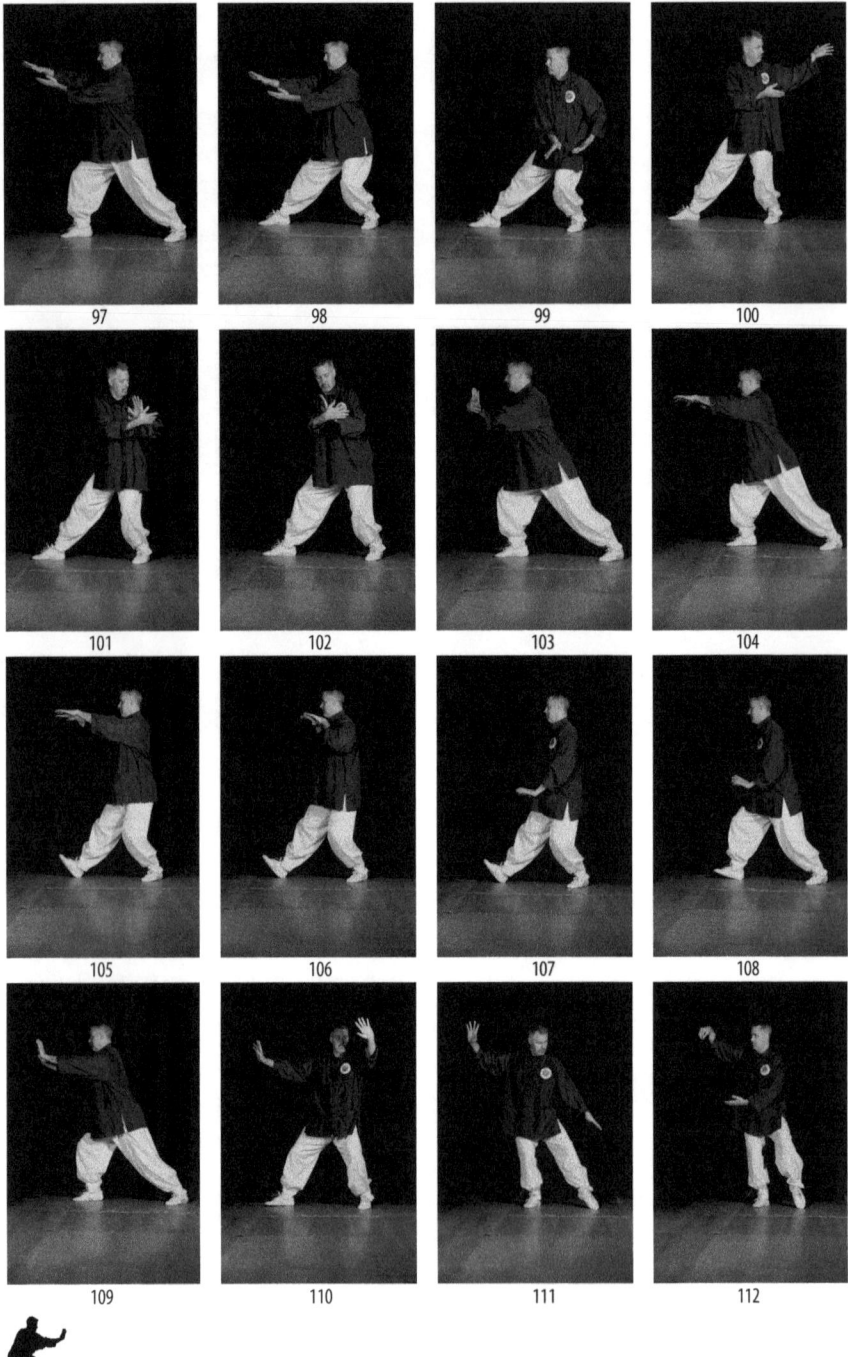

Korean Kung Fu: The Chinese Connection

97 98 99 100
101 102 103 104
105 106 107 108
109 110 111 112

82

Chapter 8. INTERNAL MARTIAL ARTS TRAINING

113 114 115 116

117 118 119 120

121 122 123 124

125 126 127 128

83

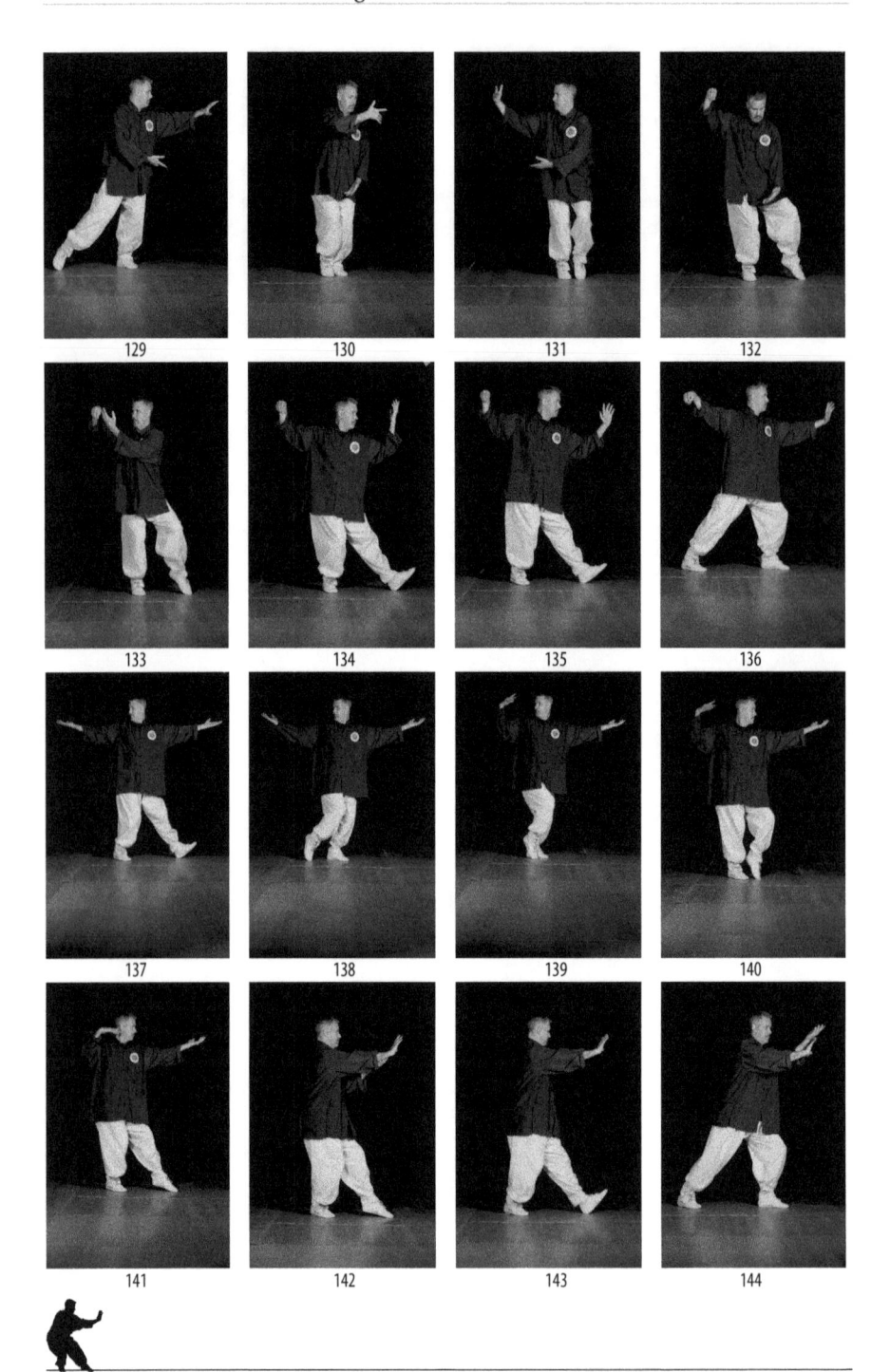

Korean Kung Fu: The Chinese Connection

129 130 131 132

133 134 135 136

137 138 139 140

141 142 143 144

84

Chapter 8. INTERNAL MARTIAL ARTS TRAINING

145 146 147 148
149 150 151 152
153 154 155 156
157 158 159 160

85

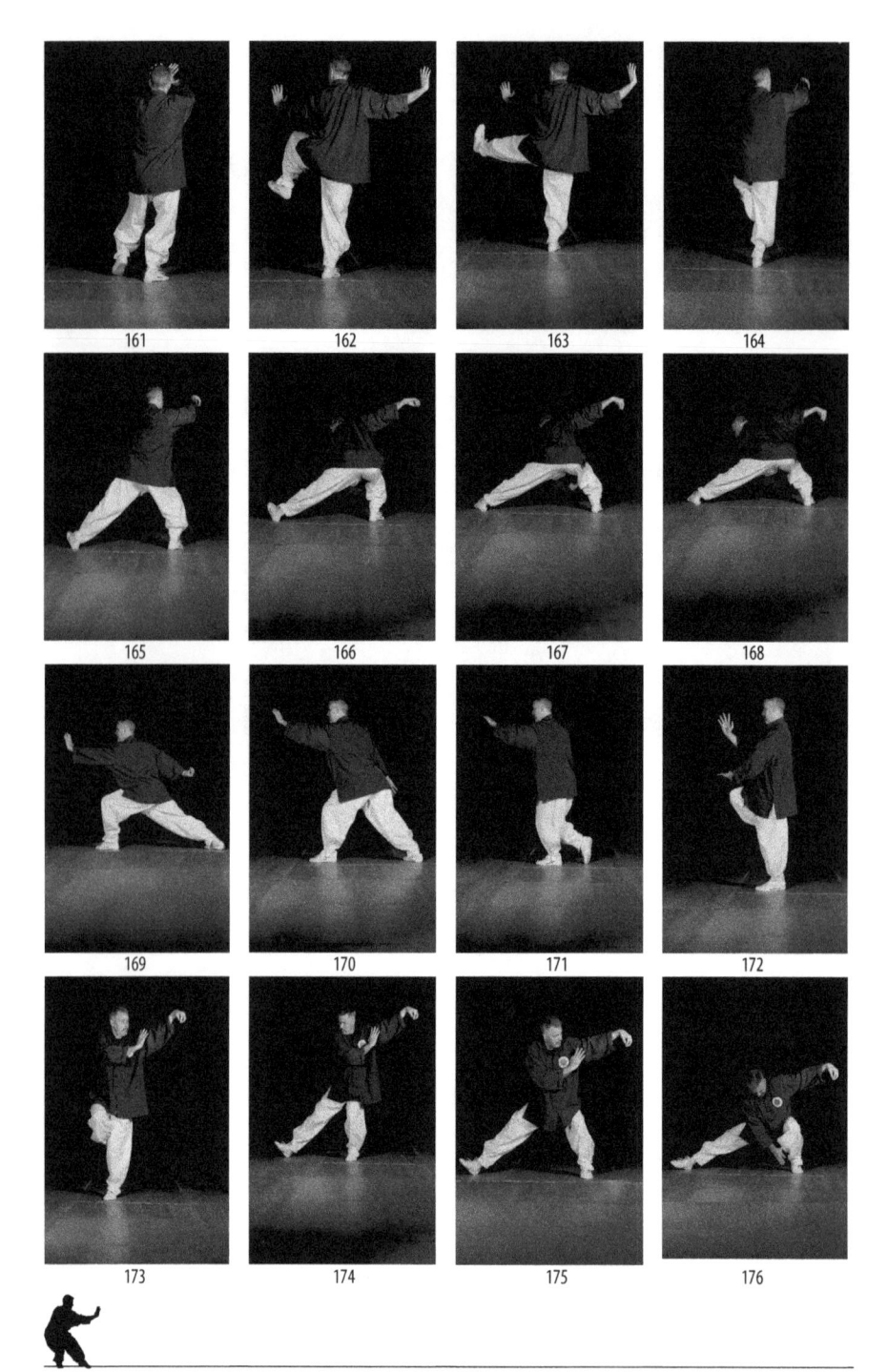

Korean Kung Fu: The Chinese Connection

161   162   163   164
165   166   167   168
169   170   171   172
173   174   175   176

86

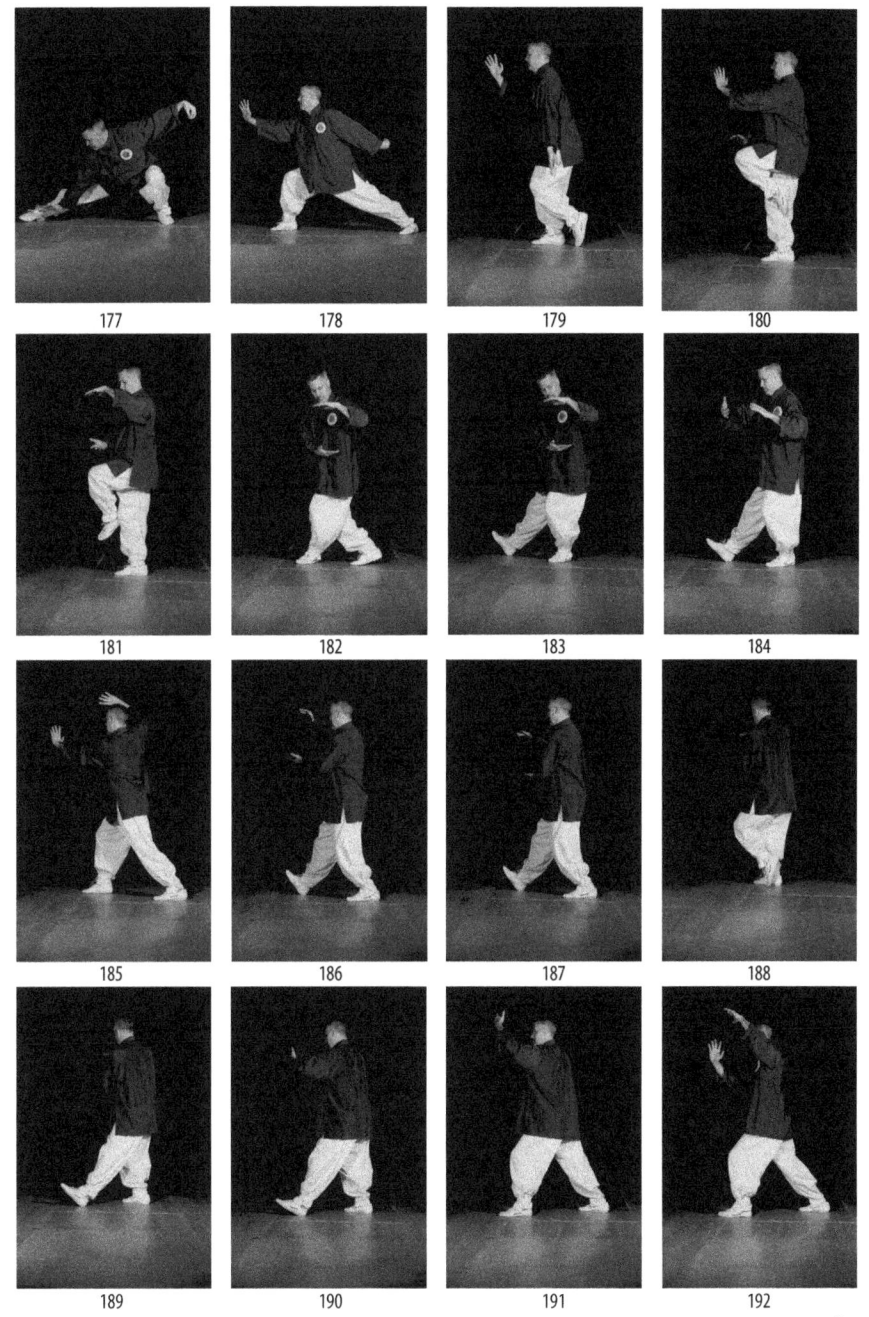

Chapter 8. INTERNAL MARTIAL ARTS TRAINING

177   178   179   180

181   182   183   184

185   186   187   188

189   190   191   192

87

Korean Kung Fu: The Chinese Connection

193 194 195 196
197 198 199 200
201 202 203 204
205 206 207 208

Chapter 8. INTERNAL MARTIAL ARTS TRAINING

209	210	211	212
213	214	215	216
217	218	219	220
221	222	223	224

Korean Kung Fu: The Chinese Connection

225   226   227   228

229   230   231   232

Chapter Nine

Kibon Ja Sae/Jiben Zi Shi
(기본자세) 基本姿勢

Basic stance practice is where all Kung Fu training begins. Korean Kung Fu schools call the practice "Kibon Ja Sae" which refers to foundation stances or elementary stances. In Chinese, it is called Jiben Zi Shi, or Chuji Bu Gung.

These stances are nearly the same in all Sip Pal Gi schools, as well as in many northern Shaolin systems around the world.

Again, there are several variations of these stances (particularly in the way in which the arms are held in the stances).

There are 7 basic stances in Sip Pal Gi, with a few additional *minor* stances that are not included in the stance set.

The 7 basic stances are:

Korean/Chinese	English	Chinese	Korean
Ki Ma Sik	Horse Stance	騎馬式	기마식
Deung San Sik	Mountain Stance	登山式	등산식
Du Li/Dok Lib Sik	Crane Stance	獨立式	독립식
Hyu/Xue Sik	Empty/Cat Stance	虛式	휴식
Tang Nang Sik	Praying Mantis Stance	螳螂式	당랑식
Jun Do Sik/Ka Hwi Sik	Scissor Stance	剪刀式	전도식
So Deung San Sik	Small Mountain Stance	小登山式	소등산식

Additionally, there is the *four-six stance* that is used frequently in the forms but not included in the basic stance set. The four-six stance is very similar to the traditional back stance in Tae Kwon Do, except that the feet are not as straight as in Tae Kwon Do, rather than the back foot being pointed at a 90 degree angle, it is closer to a 45 degree angle, and the front toes are slightly turned inward.

Four Six Stance

The word "Sik" (pronounced SHICK) is translated as "style."
In Korean language the letters s and i together are pronounced "SHE."
This is why Sip Pal Gi (also Sib Pal Gi, Sip Pal Ki) is often spelled "Ship Pal Gi."

Chapter 9. BASIC KUNG FU STANCES

THE 7 BASIC STANCES

READY

1. HORSE STANCE
Square Horse Stance

2. MOUNTAIN STANCE
Bow Stance

3. CAT STANCE
Empty Stance

4. CRANE STANCE
Single Leg Stance

5. PRAYING MANTIS STANCE
Stretching Stance

6. SCISSOR STANCE
Twisted Horse Stance

7. SMALL MOUNTAIN STANCE
Dragon Riding Stance

*Each stance should be held for 20-30 seconds and is performed on both sides.

Chapter Ten

Tan Tae/Tan Tui
(탄토이) 潭腿

After a student has learned the basic stances, the next level of training is usually Tan Tae (Tan Tui, in Chinese).

Tan Tui is the beginner level training for many Northern styles of Kung Fu and is considered the backbone of these particular systems. It is said that if a student's Tan Tui is good then his Kung Fu is good.

An interesting note: As masters grow older, they often abandon practice of the longer forms in favor of practicing the Tan Tui sets, solely, as they contain all the basic elements needed to keep sharp as a Kung Fu practitioner.

Although there are many variations, there are generally two distinct sets of Tan Tui (also called Tam Toi).

These are the 10 Road Set and the 12 Road Set.

Each one of the Tan Tui is called a "road." They are simply very short forms (ranging between 3 and 6 movements in total) that are repeated up and down the room (thus the term "road"). They can also be practiced in a circle with larger groups or they can be practiced individually as a warm up.

The 12 Road set is the more widely practiced by many Northern Kung Fu schools and is usually associated with the Chin Woo Association (created by famed martial arts master Huo Yuan Jia, the character that Jet Li portrayed in the 2006 movie, Fearless). Many of the Korean Kung Fu systems in Korea have a connection with the Chin Woo Asscociation.

Huo Yuan Jia/ Jo Yun Hwa (Korean)
(Circa 1898)

Each road is comprised of a series of stances, blocks, strikes, footwork, and kicks.

Tan Tui is considered to be a complete system all on its own, but is commonly used as the first series of basic forms for styles like Chang Chuan (Long Fist).

Practicing Tan Tui will improve fighting skills, balance, strength, stamina, and focus. The Tan Tui forms contain all the basic skills and several agility drills required to learn the advanced forms.

In some Schools, Tan Tui is taught as the first set of moving forms, since they are simple and repetitive, to build the skills

Chapter 10. TAN TUI

necessary to advance in the system.

Tan Tui can trace its roots back to China's Hui Muslim community, particularly the 10 road set. They were adopted by the Chinese early on and used as an integral part of training in Northern Kung Fu systems.

Each set of movements also contain valuable self-defense applications and should not be overlooked. The *essence* of each system of Kung Fu can be garnered through practicing the Tan Tui sets.

One may choose to practice a single Tan Tui road, repetitively, or practice the entire set, one after another, in reps of 8-10 each before moving on to the next one (or doing as many reps as it takes to get from one side of the room to the other, and then coming back to the beginning location with either the same Tan Tui, or by doing the next Tan Tui in the series.)

It should be noted that attention should be paid to strong stances while performing Tan Tui, as well as good strong basic blocks, strikes and kicks, since the habits one develops in practicing the Tan Tui will carry over into how the more advanced forms are performed.

Kung Fu is considered an *art* as well as a discipline, so Tan Tui should also look artistic and beautiful while helping the student develop power, speed, accuracy, balance, and cardiovascular conditioning.

In the art of Sip Pal Gi there are some slight distinctions, particularly in the kicks, which have been influenced by other Korean kicking arts, such as Tae Kwon Do and Tang Soo Do.

Also, where, in many Chinese systems they will use what is known as a "rolling back fist," their Korean counterparts will use more of an inner forearm block or strike (basically the same movement, but more of an emphasis on attacking "inward," rather than downward, as if to be using the forearm to strike at an opponent's shin bone).

Regular practice of Tan Tui will greatly enhance a practitioner's stamina and is one heck of a cardio workout, *even* if only performing half of them, (and *without* focusing on low, stances and powerful kicks and strikes).

As a rule of thumb, the kicks in Tan Tui are to be performed below the waist, and even as low as knee-height.

In recent years, many Kung Fu schools around the world, including many Sip Pal Gi schools, have replaced the Tan Tui practice with the more modern Wushu basics.

On the next several pages we will view the 12 Tan Tui roads in their entirety.

Chapter 10. TAN TUI

Tan Tui #1

1. BOW

2. READY

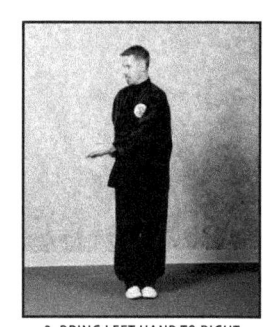

3. BRING LEFT HAND TO RIGHT WAIST

4. STEP OUT TO LEFT

5. SHIFT TO MOUNTAIN STANCE

6. RIGHT PUNCH

7. LEFT PUNCH

8. RIGHT PUNCH

Tan Tui #2

1. BOW

2. READY

3. RIGHT PALM BLOCK TO LEFT WAIST

4. STEP OUT TO LEFT

5. LEFT MOUNTAIN STANCE LEFT PUNCH

6. RIGHT PUNCH

7. LEFT PUNCH RIGHT KICK

Chapter 10. TAN TUI

Tan Tui #3

1. BOW/SALUTE

2. READY

3. RIGHT PALM BLOCK TO LEFT WAIST

4. STEP OUT TO LEFT

5. HORSE STANCE LEFT PUNCH

6. SHIFT TO MOUNTAIN STANCE RIGHT PUNCH

7. SHIFT BACK TO HORSE STANCE LEFT PUNCH

Tan Tui #4

1. BOW/SALUTE

2. READY

3. RIGHT PALM BLOCK TO LEFT WAIST

4. STEP OUT TO LEFT

5. LEFT HORSE STANCE LEFT PUNCH

6. MOUNTAIN STANCE OPEN LEFT PALM

7. RIGHT ELBOW INTO LEFT PALM

8. EXTEND ARMS

9. PULL ARMS TO WAIST RIGHT KICK

Chapter 10. TAN TUI

Tan Tui #5

1. BOW/SALUTE

2. READY

3. RIGHT PALM BLOCK TO LEFT WAIST

4. STEP OUT TO LEFT

5. LEFT MOUNTAIN STANCE LEFT PUNCH

6. PULL BACK TO CRANE STANCE BRING ARMS TO REAR

7. STEP FORWARD TO MOUNTAIN STANCE, LEFT HAMMER FIST STRIKE

8. STEP FORWARD, RIGHT HAMMER FIST STRIKE

9. FROM SAME STANCE, LEFT HAMMER FIST STRIKE (PENETRATE DEEPER)

103

Tan Tui #6

1. BOW/SALUTE

2. READY

3. RIGHT PALM BLOCK TO LEFT WAIST

4. STEP OUT TO LEFT

5. LEFT MOUNTAIN STANCE LEFT PUNCH

6. PULL BACK TO CRANE STANCE, ARMS TO REAR

7. STEP FORWARD TO MOUNTAIN STANCE, LEFT HAMMER FIST STRIKE

8. STEP FORWARD, RIGHT HAMMER FIST STRIKE, CONTINUE FIST DOWN PAST WAIST

9. OPEN RIGHT HAND TO BLOCK AND CATCH, BRING LEFT FIST TO WAIST

Chapter 10. TAN TUI

Tan Tui #6 (cont'd)

10. RIGHT ARM CIRCLES UP TO KNIFE HAND BLOCK

11. PULL RIGHT FIST TO WAIST, LEFT VERTICAL PUNCH

Tan Tui #7

1. BOW/SALUTE
2. READY 
3. RIGHT PALM BLOCK TO LEFT WAIST 
4. STEP OUT TO LEFT 
5. LEFT MOUNTAIN STANCE LEFT PUNCH 
6. LEFT UPPER BLOCK RIGHT VERTICAL PUNCH 
7. RIGHT ARM BLOCKS DOWN AND ACROSS TO LEFT 
8. RIGHT KICK

Chapter 10. TAN TUI

Tan Tui #8

1. BOW/SALUTE
2. READY 
3. RIGHT PALM BLOCK TO LEFT WAIST 
4. STEP OUT TO LEFT 
5. HORSE STANCE SIDE PUNCH 
6. SHIFT TO MOUNTAIN STANCE RIGHT PUNCH 
7. RIGHT KICK LEFT PUNCH 
8. BEFORE RIGHT KICK LANDS, KICK WITH LEFT AND PUNCH WITH RIGHT (DOUBLE KICK) 

SPECIAL NOTATION:
#8 can be performed as single kicks or double jumping kicks—very similar to a Tae Kwon Do double roundhouse kick used in Olympic sparring.

107

Tan Tui #9

1. BOW/SALUTE

2. READY

3. RIGHT PALM BLOCK TO LEFT WAIST

4. STEP OUT TO LEFT

5. MOUNTAIN STANCE LEFT PUNCH

6. SHIFT TO REAR MOUNTAIN STANCE LEFT PRESSING BLOCK

7. RIGHT UPPER CUT LEFT ARM TO REAR

8. STRIKE RIGHT WRIST WITH LEFT INNER WRIST/FOREARM

9. SHIFT BACK TO FRONT, SWING LEFT ARM ACROSS TO LEFT, RIGHT DOWNWARD HAMMER FIST

Chapter 10. TAN TUI

Tan Tui #9 (cont'd)

10. RIGHT INWARD FOREARM BLOCK

11. RIGHT KICK
LEFT ARM STILL OUT TO SIDE

Tan Tui #10

1. BOW/SALUTE

2. READY

3. RIGHT PALM BLOCK TO LEFT WAIST

4. STEP OUT TO LEFT

5. HORSE STANCE SIDE PUNCH

6. SLIDE LEFT FOOT BACK TO CAT STANCE LEFT UPPER BLOCK

7. FROM SAME POSITION RIGHT UPPER BLOCK REACH OUT WITH LEFT FOOT (CRAB STEP)

8. SETTLE IN HORSE STANCE SIDE PUNCH

Chapter 10. TAN TUI

Tan Tui #11

1. BOW/SALUTE

2. READY

3. RIGHT PALM BLOCK TO LEFT WAIST

4. STEP OUT TO LEFT

5. MOUNTAIN STANCE LEFT PUNCH

6. SHIFT TO HORSE STANCE PULL ARMS TO REAR

7. SHIFT BACK TO MOUNTAIN STANCE LEFT LOW BLOCK, RIGHT UPWARD STRIKE TO GROIN

8. RIGHT INWARD FOREARM BLOCK ACROSS BODY LEFT ARM OUT TO SIDE

9. FRONT SNAP KICK LEFT ARM STAYS TO SIDE

Tan Tui #12

1. BOW/SALUTE

2. READY

3. HOP ONTO LEFT LEG
LEFT MANTIS CATCH

4. RIGHT LEG STEPS FORWARD
RIGHT INNER FOREARM STRIKE TO
LEFT HAND (THUMBLESS GRIP)

5. LIFT LEFT KNEE
REACH WITH BOTH HANDS TO
RIGHT, OPEN HANDS

6. PULL BACK TO HORSE STANCE
LEFT FIST TO WAIST, RIGHT
INNER FOREARM BLOCK

7. QUICKLY SPRING FORWARD
RIGHT UPPER BLOCK,
LEFT VERTICAL PUNCH

8. REACH OUT WITH BOTH HANDS

9. PULL FISTS TO WAIST
FRONT SNAP KICK

Chapter Eleven

Iron Body Conditioning
(철포삼)鐵布衫

An important part of many external styles of Kung Fu (and some internal styles) is Iron Body conditioning.

Each style has its own set of conditioning drills used to increase pain tolerance levels and to allow the practitioner to strike an object at full force without injury to himself.

One of the most popular Iron Body exercises for the arms is called 3-Star arm conditioning. 3-Star arm conditioning (often called Pe Ken Derrien/Dalyun in Korean circles, or Da Sahm Sung, which means "3 Star Striking") helps to develop the areas on the arm used for many blocks and strikes.

 3-Star arm conditioning can be done with a partner or alone, against a solid object such as a tree or a pole (either wooden or metal).

Care must be taken in the beginning stages so as to not overdo it.

When beginning, the practitioner should begin striking the areas lightly at first (in a slow rhythmical manner), striking with the inner forearm first (just below where a watch would be worn, about an inch up from the wrist) and then the outer forearm (at the same location but on the opposite side of the arm), then once more on the same side. There are 3 strikes in total and it should be performed like a *strike*.

So, to help the reader visualize this, think of striking an opponent in the ribs using the inner forearm, next, bring the same arm up and strike the opponent in the neck with the outer forearm, then come back down and strike the opponent in the ribs once more with the outer forearm.

Korean Kung Fu: The Chinese Connection

3 Star Conditioning

1. RELAXED HORSE STANCE STRIKE RIGHT INNER WRISTS TOGETHER

2. TURN WAIST TO LEFT SAME ARM

3. TURN WAIST BACK TO RIGHT, SAME ARM STRIKES AT TOP (BACKS OF WRISTS OR BOTTOM)

4. TURN WAIST TO LEFT (SAME ARM)

5. SAME WRIST, STRIKE DOWN WITH BOTTOM OF WRIST

6. STRIKE LEFT ARMS TOGETHER (SAME AS IN FIGURE 1)

7. STRIKE LEFT WRISTS AT TOP (SAME AS IN FIGURE 3)

8. TURN WAIST TO RIGHT

9. STRIKE DOWNWARD WITH LEFT WRISTS, (LOW BLOCK)

Chapter 11. IRON BODY CONDITIONING

CLOSE-UP OF INNER WRIST/ FOREARM STRIKE
Star 1

CLOSE-UP OF BACK OF WRIST STRIKE
Star 2

CLOSE-UP OF OUTER/BOTTOM WRIST STRIKE
Star 3

The above illustrations show the 3 different "stars," which are simply 3 different areas of the wrist. It is important to develop all of the areas of the arms for powerful and effective blocks and strikes while minimizing damage to your own arm during combat.

As you progress, add a little more power to each strike, gradually, until you can strike with full power and not feel pain.

This practice helps the bones in the area to grow thicker and be able to handle more pressure, while de-sensitizing the nerves in that area.

After training it is good to use a strong Chinese herbal liniment to aid in healing the area. There are many to choose from but one of the best liniments is popularly called *Dit Da Jow* ("Hit Wine", in Cantonese).

After a rigorous Iron-Body practice, simply douse a paper towel with the liquid and apply it to the areas needed (holding the towel in place for a couple of minutes, or taping the towel to your skin using sports tape so that the Jow can penetrate deeper).

A second method is to prepare a small pot with the Jow in it and dip your hands into it and allow them to soak for a couple of minutes.

Allow the area to dry and then reapply the liniment once again. There are many different types of Dit Da Jow available and the buyer should take care in choosing a suitable Jow for personal use. There are several places on the internet that one can find high-quality Dit Da Jow. Jows that are stored in dark brown glass jars are best. Avoid those shipped in plastic containers as the plastic melts away from the bottle and can change the compound of the Jow and make it less effective.

Some of the better liniments can actually dissolve a bruise nearly immediately.

The knuckles of the hand may also be developed in this manner.

To do this, find a firm object (the Japanese use what is known as a "Makiwara" board– a piece of wood covered in braided thread to soften the surface *just a bit*) or a canvas bag filled with beans, sand, pebbles, rocks, bb's, etc… and begin striking it with the knuckles (either with an open handed back hand slap or a solid fist, using a punch.)

As you progress, strike a little harder and deeper with each blow. Practice can begin with 5 or 10 strikes and continue up to 100 or 1000 strikes each day.

Using this conditioning to protect the *torso* is called "Iron Shirt" training and allows the practitioner to receive full power kicks and strikes to the torso without any damage.

One can use Iron Body Training to train virtually any area of the body to develop the area into a weapon or to allow the practitioner to absorb a full power blow with little to no injury.

Chapter 11. IRON BODY CONDITIONING

Iron Body Training is enhanced with Iron Shirt Qi Gong (Qigong) exercises in which postures are held, and special breathing exercises are used, to increase Ki flow, along with "packing" and "wrapping" of the internal organs with Ki energy.

Additionally, many systems of Kung Fu use special *2-Man Set* drills that have a secondary purpose of conditioning various areas of the body for combative use.

Northern Praying Mantis systems use these sets as a large part of their training regimen. In addition to the Iron Body conditioning that happens, these exercises also serve to increase hand-eye coordination, stamina and mental-strength conditioning.

Practitioners of Sip Pal Gi engage in regular iron body training on the areas of the wrist where a watchband would be worn, as this is a very important *weapon*, used in the system, and included in the majority of the forms in the system.

In fact, many of the forms have *built-in* iron body training components included, which allow a student to slowly begin to develop more power until they can strike themselves at full power without leaving a bruise on their arm.

The sound of these strikes, once a student achieves the advanced levels, is amazing to hear.

The power from these strikes gives an onlooker the impression that the practitioner has so much power that he could easily break bones with it, which invokes a sense of fear into an opponent who may, after seeing this, decide that he does not wish to pursue picking a fight any longer.

Chapter Twelve

Kwon Bup Derrien/Quan Fa Duilian
(권법대련)拳法對練

In this chapter we will take a look at some of the 2-man sets of our system. These sets are used to bridge the gap between solo forms practice and self-defense. Each pattern has a certain amount of movements that are performed with a partner and then looped into a continuous practice that can go anywhere from 30 seconds to 5 minutes or more.

These sets help to develop several attributes at once. The first thing that will be improved by practicing these is how to modify specific techniques from the forms for use against a live opponent. This in itself is highly valuable and is something that was part of many earlier systems of Korean martial arts, but were removed for whatever reason. My guess is that many of these 2-man practice sets were probably removed when Americans began learning the arts, as a way of watering down the training a bit for the Americans, and eventually, to make the arts more interesting to the more modern generation by replacing a lot of 2-man practice with sports-oriented free sparring and one and three-step sparring techniques. I suspect that some masters removed them because of the number of injuries that students in the more modern commercial schools sustained; which would have likely caused many students to drop out.

Practicing these sets will cause bruising and pain, but with continued practice, the skin and bones become stronger and the practitioner is able to strike and block with more power without injury to himself. While the Koreans that I trained with have not used Dit Da Jow (hit wine) to help heal their injuries, the Chinese are renowned for using these herbs in their martial arts training. It could be that the Chinese purposely kept the herbal formulas a secret as a way of withholding information from the Koreans. Grandmaster Na, for example, has arms of steel and has those large white calluses on his knuckles, but has never used the herbal healing formula.

I personally recommend using a good Dit Da Jow after any extended two-man set practice, as it will help heal the injuries much faster and will help to tone up the skin and bones in those areas much faster as well, which will allow a practitioner to train more frequently and with more intensity, leading to better and faster results.

Another benefit of training with 2-man sets is increased timing. Even though both parties already know what's coming and, for the most part, *when* it's coming, there is still a different rhythm to each partner, and this will serve to improve the timing skills of both practitioners.

Then, there are the cardiovascular benefits. Practice just 30 seconds of a 2-man set and you can become easily winded. With continued, consistent practice, however, stamina levels will increase dramatically.

Doing 2-man set training is a bit different from doing solo forms training, in that you encounter resistance to each movement, whereas, with an empty hand form you do not. So, there is a strength-building benefit to the practice as well.

The very first 2-man set is known as "8 Step" or "Pal Bo" in Korean. This set is comprised of 8 individual movements that loop back into the first motion again, once the 8th motion is completed.

In order for the pattern to work with a partner, person "A" must initiate *movement number one* in an offensive manner, while partner "B" executes movement number "5." The speed can be varied, from very slow, where much attention is paid to the exactness of each stance and technique, to very, very fast, in which the partners pay much less attention to the exactness of their stances and techniques. Another method of performing these sets is to use *stickiness,* where each technique thrown at your opponent is resisted, and there is a feeling of *sticking* to your opponent's limb as he kicks or punches.

The Korean term sometimes used for this type of training is called Deta, or "Promised Sparring."

Pal Bo Derrien/Ba Bu Duilian (8-Step Sparring)

1. READY

2. BOW TO PARTNER

3. ATTACKER STEPS BACK TO READY

4. ATTACKER THROWS FRONT SNAP KICK

5. DEFENDER STEPS BACK TO HORSE STANCE

6. DEFENDER PREPARES BLOCK

7. DEFENDER BLOCKS KICK WITH LOW BLOCK

8. ATTACKER PUNCHES TO FACE

Chapter 12. 2-MAN TRAINING

9. DEFENDER AVOIDS

10. DEFENDER BLOCKS PUNCH & GRABS WRIST

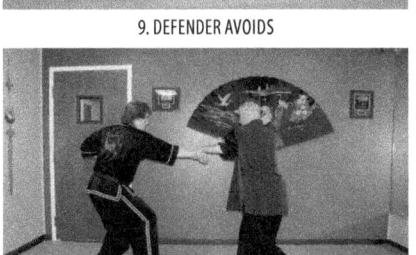

11. DEFENDER TWIST, PULLS AND STEPS FORWARD

12. DEFENDER ATTACKS NECK

13. ATTACKER BLOCKS ATTACK WITH LEFT ARM

14. ATTACKER PREPARES TO BLOCK

15. DEFENDER PUNCHES TO RIBS

16. ATTACKER BLOCKS PUNCH TO RIBS

Korean Kung Fu: The Chinese Connection

17. DEFENDER PREPARES TO KICK

18. DEFENDER KICKS
(Repeating), Now, Defender Becomes Attacker

19. ATTACKER BLOCKS KICK WITH LOW BLOCK

20. ATTACKER PREPARES TO PUNCH FACE

21. ATTACKER PUNCHES FACE

22. DEFENDER PREPARES TO GRAB PUNCH

23. DEFENDER GRABS PUNCH

24. DEFENDER TWIST TO PREPARE STRIKE TO NECK

Chapter 12. 2-MAN TRAINING

25. DEFENDER STRIKES TO NECK

26. ATTACKER BLOCKS STRIKE WITH LEFT HAND

27. DEFENDER RELEASES GRAB FROM ARM (PREPARES TO PUNCH)

28. DEFENDER THROWS PUNCH TO RIBS

29. ATTACKER BLOCKS PUNCH WITH LOW BLOCK

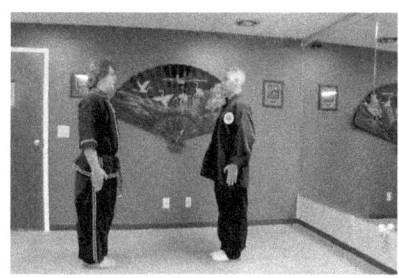

30. RETURN TO ATTENTION POSITION

31. BOW AND END

Pal Bo Derrien Yi Dan/Ba Bu Dui Lian Er Duan (8-Step #2)

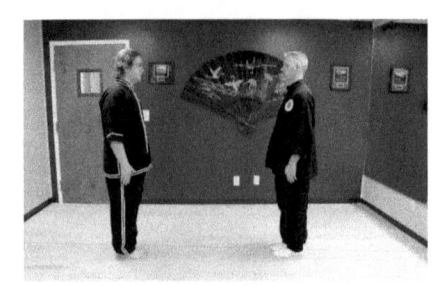

1. ATTENTION

2. BOW/SALUTE

3. READY

4. ATTACKER STEPS BACK TO READY

5. DEFENDER STEPS BACK TO AVOID KICK

6. DEFENDER BLOCKS KICK WITH LOW BLOCK

7. ATTACKER PUNCHES TO DEFENDER'S FACE

8. DEFENDER CATCHES PUNCH AND PULLS

Chapter 12. 2-MAN TRAINING

9. DEFENDER STEPS FORWARD AND STRIKES AT HEAD WITH INNER FOREARM STRIKE, ATTACKER LEANS BACK AND DUCKS

10. DEFENDER PREPARES TO THROW RIGHT UPPERCUT

11. DEFENDER UPPER CUTS, ATTACKER BLOCKS UPPERCUT WITH DOWNWARD OUTER FOREARM BLOCK (ASSISTED WITH LEFT HAND COVERING THE RIGHT WRIST WITH A THUMBLESS GRIP))

12. ROLES CHANGE (PERSON ON RIGHT BECOMES THE ATTACKER) DEFENDER SKIPS BACK (RIGHT LEG CROSSES IN FRONT OF LEFT) AS DEFENDER PREPARES TO KICK

13. DEFENDER BLOCKS FRONT KICK FROM ATTACKER

14. DEFENDER CATCHES PUNCH

15. DEFENDER STEPS FORWARD AND EXECUTES LEFT INNER FOREARM STRIKE TO DEFENDER'S NECK, ATTACKER LEANS AND DUCKS

16. DEFENDER RELEASES GRIP ON WRIST AND PREPARES TO UPPERCUT, ATTACKER PREPARES TO BLOCK UPPERCUT

17. DEFENDER EXECUTES UPPER CUT TO RIBS ATTACKER BLOCKS UPPERCUT, ASSISTED BLOCK

18. ATTACKER SKIPS BACK TO PREPARE TO BLOCK ON-COMING KICK FROM DEFENDER

19. ATTACKER CONTINUES TO MOVE AWAY FROM KICK

20. ATTACKER LANDS IN HORSE STANCE AFTER SKIP AND BLOCKS KICK WITH DOWNWARD OUTER FOREARM BLOCK (ASSISTED)

21. BOW/SALUTE

There are several other sets that are practiced in our system as well, but these are the 2 most common sets. While the pictures show only one basic performance, these sets should be practiced repeatedly for several rotations before finishing and bowing.

The sets should begin slowly and then increase in speed little by little until both partners are moving very quickly. Additionally, after both partners are warmed up properly and the techniques are flowing nicely, try applying a little pressure to each kick, block and strike to give your partner some resistance.

This will help develop your internal power and teach you to move with purpose, rather than simply performing a "routine."

Chapter Thirteen

Tu Ro/Tao Lu
(투로)套路

Tu Ro, or "forms" training (Taolu, in Chinese, also known as Hyung or Poomse in Korean) is the most important part of the training regimen in the majority of Kung Fu schools.

Forms training offers a complete mind/body training practice for the student. Regular training in forms leads to better coordination, control, speed, intensity, balance, accuracy, hand-eye coordination, increased stamina, strength and cardiovascular improvement.

Forms were originally designed to catalog specific self-defense techniques, and/or skills, in an organized and scientific sequence.

Many of the self-defense applications were purposely hidden in the forms to keep enemies from learning their secrets and to make it difficult for the average person to decipher their meanings.

Once a practitioner realizes what a technique (or a series or techniques) mean, their training moves to another level and their understanding of the application of the techniques shows in their performance.

There are generally one or two different self-defense applications for each technique and one or more *hidden* applications that can only be learned by studying with a qualified Master; as these hidden applications are passed down from teacher to student over many generations.

A form is like a make-believe fighting scenario, in which the practitioner is mentally and physically engaged in mortal combat with one attacker, or possibly multiple attackers.

The forms in a particular system will share many of the same basics found in that particular system's Tan Tui and basic stance forms.

There are <u>3 phases</u> a student should progress through when learning a form.

The first phase is the <u>memorization phase</u>. During this phase, the student simply runs through the form repeatedly to develop the basic skeleton of the pattern, paying little attention to how *proper* everything is.

Once the student has memorized the entire pattern, he should move to phase two in his training, which is the <u>phase of corrections</u>.

During this phase, the student should focus heavily on proper mechanics and execution of each technique, with less thought devoted to power or speed.

A student never really leaves this phase for the duration of his/her career in the martial arts.

Once significant development in phase two has taken place, the student enters the third phase of training, which is the <u>performance phase</u>, which means to bring the form *to* life.

Once the student enters into the 3rd phase of learning, he will rotate back and forth between phase 2 and phase 3 as he learns, through performing, where improvements or corrections are needed.

Each form is created with a certain energy, speed and cadence.

Chapter 13. FORMS TRAINING

It is designed to elicit a certain spirit from the practitioner.

It is the student's job to find these various energies and cadences, through rigorous practice of the form, with much thought given to intensity and power.

Every performance of a form should be governed by 6 principles:

The 3 C's (Clean, Crisp and Clear) and the S.P.I. Principle (Speed, Power and Intensity).

Eye contact and intent is also very important in Kung Fu forms training. The eyes should be directed toward the enemy (usually at the end of one's fist or foot) and should not wander during a performance.

One should maintain a serious gaze throughout the performance and deliver techniques both with smoothness and continuity while using "Fa Jing" (explosive power) in strikes and kicks.

At certain points in some forms there are what are known as "Spirit Yells" or "Energy Shouts." Koreans call this a "Kihap" and Japanese call it a "Kiai"- which means, *energy coordination*. "Qi He" (pronounced Chi Huh) or "Fa Sheng (pronounced "Fah Shung") are the Chinese terms for it. These points in the form are where the most energy is spent.

At these points in a form this is often coupled with a brief pause (both for aesthetic appearance and for timing and control).

Once the student has practiced properly for some time he will be able to "step outside" of himself and almost literally *observe*, from a 3rd-party perspective, how the form looks to a viewer.

Time appears to slow down and the practitioner is better

able to fix things *on the fly* during a performance.

This phase is the final phase of "mastering" a form. It is said that it takes a minimum of three years to master a single form. For some of the more advanced forms it can take much longer.

Due to the complexity of Kung Fu forms, in comparison to Tang Soo Do or Tae Kwon Do forms, it can take longer to achieve a black sash in Kung Fu than to achieve a black *belt* in arts like Karate or Tae Kwon Do, and why it takes a *lifetime* to truly master the martial arts.

The number of forms in various Kung Fu systems varies widely. Some systems teach the Tan Tuis as the first form and then only 5 or 6 longer forms after that, as well as a handful of weapons forms.

Other systems teach one or two forms per rank up to the Black Sash level and then teach multiple longer forms after Black Sash, and, in addition, up to 18 separate weapons forms, as well.

Modern Wushu tends to place a stronger emphasis on aesthetic movement that is *pleasing to the eye* than most other martial arts, since the art is also considered the National Sport of China, and many of the forms were created in the middle of the 20th century between 1950 and 1980 by using existing traditional styles of forms and adding elements from gymnastics and ballet to make them more exciting and challenging for the practitioner and more exciting for audiences.

The forms of Modern Wushu continue to evolve each year, while traditional Kung Fu systems focus on more practical movements and less flashy techniques; although, compared to arts such as Karate or Tae Kwon Do, some of the techniques found in traditional Kung Fu can be termed as "flashy" in their own right.

Chapter 13. FORMS TRAINING

In traditional Kung Fu, depending on the teacher, a bit less attention may be paid to *perfect* hand positions, body postures and stances than in Modern Wushu, which is why some training in Modern Wushu by a traditional Kung Fu practitioner can be very valuable.

My personal opinion is that Martial Artists don't train *solely* for fighting. They also train to improve themselves mentally, physically, emotionally and spiritually.

Forms training is training in *artistic movement* and, as such, can help a person achieve artistic expression through the movements in forms, as well as to learn the "essence" of that particular martial art and many of that art's most effective self-defense techniques and skills.

Forms training has been around for thousands of years. It has benefited thousands of people and it will be around for many more thousands of years to follow.

Martial arts is comprised of two words—Martial (war/military) Art (beauty). Sparring and self-defense training take care of the war/fighting part, while forms training makes the practice truly an *art*, and adds to the fighting skills of the practitioner, while conditioning the body and mind.

The forms training varies from system to system; some are very basic in nature while some are very complex and take years to master.

While the forms of Sip Pal Gi are fairly basic in nature, compared to many Contemporary Wushu forms, as the forms of Sip Pal Gi forms are fairly simplistic. However, compared to many Karate, Tae Kwon Do or Tang Soo Do forms, they can be considered quite challenging; particularly those forms with a heavier praying mantis influence in them.

The arts of Shotokan Karate, Tang Soo Do, and Tae Kwon Do can trace their lineage back to Northern Long Fist Kung Fu. Several of the older forms taught in traditional Tae Kwon Do or Tang Soo Do draw their roots from Sip Pal Gi. Some of these forms are *So Ho Yun, Sorim Jang Kwon* (a basic 2-man fighting form that was taught in many Tang Soo Do and Tae Kwon Do schools in the 1960's and 1970's), Dan Kwon, Pal Ki Kwon, along with the *Chil Sung* forms and *Yuk Ro* forms created by Grandmaster Hwang Kee.

It's also interesting to note that the words "Tang Soo" (as in Tang Soo Do) originally meant "China Hand" in homage to the Chinese martial art of Kung Fu.

Now, in fairness, Tang Soo Do has also been heavily influenced by the Japanese arts, and is the Korean art that most closely resembles Japanese Karate.

Another interesting point is that the term "Karate" was *also* originally translated as "China Hand," but was later *changed* by Gichin Funakoshi (founder of Shotokan Karate- a near direct lineage to Tang Soo Do) to be translated as "Empty Hand." You can change names, but you can't change history.

The Okinawans and Japanese practitioners took what was taught to them by the *Chinese*, simplified it and then made it very linear and rigid to better reflect their culture.

Simply compare the cultural differences and you will see how it all fits together.

If you listen to a person who speaks fluent Chinese you will hear a very relaxed, flowing language. You will see a very relaxed atmosphere in many schools owned and operated by Chinese masters.

Chapter 13. FORMS TRAINING

Chinese practitioners wear shoes during their training and students often dress in simple t-shirts and baggy pants, which is quite the opposite of Japanese, Korean and Okinawan cultures.

Listen to a Japanese person speak and you will hear short, powerful words, spoken with strictness. You will see very prim and proper etiquette and social behavior. Inside their Dojos you will see plain white uniforms, hard wood floors and no shoes.

A culture of hierarchy and seniority is observed in the Japanese culture that is very firm and strict, just like their martial art of Karate.

You will notice a very similar atmosphere in Okinawan schools and more traditional Korean-operated martial arts schools.

Korean language is *also* very "staccato" in tonality, much like the Japanese, although a little bit less so.

So, their martial arts are a direct reflection of their culture.

From my personal experiences and study of the martial arts, as a whole, I have come to the conclusion (although it is still just an educated guess, based on my own personal experiences) that all arts originated from Kung Fu.

It is my opinion that Kung Fu is the most complete and comprehensive of all martial arts and that, somewhere in history; different arts were derived from the various Kung Fu systems in practice today.

For instance, the Chinese Kung Fu system of Shui Jiao (摔跤), which is a component of Kung Fu taught in many schools, is the *original* art that influenced the arts of Judo and Jiu-Jitsu.

I believe that, somewhere along the line, a practitioner of a Kung Fu style that practiced Shui Jiao as part of their sparring practice formally "extracted" this practice and built an entire system based solely on that practice alone.

This eventually became the art of Jiu-Jitsu, which was further dissected, by Jigoro Kano and turned into the "sport" of Judo (which is essentially Jiu Jitsu with all of the joint locks and dangerous breaking techniques removed).

I believe that, somewhere along the line, a Kung Fu practitioner found that he really enjoyed the practice of Chin 'Na (擒拿), which means "Seize and Control," and his passion was in this "particular" part of his training; allowing him to excel in it and then he isolated it from the other parts of his training to come up with the arts that we now know as *Aikido* and *Hapkido*.

One look at any Chin 'Na technique and it's easy to see the correlation between the arts, and since China's culture is historically much older than both Korea or Japan, things had to *begin* somewhere.

This type of thing has continued to happen through the ages and has most recently happened with the art of Tae Kwon Do.

Many more modern Tae Kwon Do schools have, for all intents and purposes, done away with much of the self-defense training and the traditional practice of forms, in favor of the development of the more modern "Olympic-Style" of Tae Kwon Do which is taught as a sport than a self-defense system.

If you look at the *real* history of Tae Kwon Do, the art was not "officially" created until around the mid 1950's and went through many name changes and transitional stages until recently.

Chapter 13. FORMS TRAINING

This was primarily due to the Japanese influence in the art that was a direct result of the Japanese occupation of Korea up to the point of their defeat in World War II.

From 1910-1945, the Japanese government forbid the Koreans from practicing their own martial arts and burned their history books, in an attempt to make them part of Japan and to force the Koreans to adopt the Japanese culture.

When the war ended the Koreans were left with many Japanese-influenced customs and arts.

During the time of the Japanese occupation of Korea many Japanese masters took on Korean students and taught them their systems.

Once the Japanese were defeated and Korea was freed, it wasn't long before the Koreans attempted to regain their own identities, particularly in the area of martial arts.

Back in the 1960's and 70's, when many Korean masters migrated to the United States, there were very few *Tae Kwon Do* schools.

The majority of these schools were known as "Korean Karate" schools, and their signage reflected this.

The majority of these schools taught Japanese forms (Kata) that were given Korean names and slightly modified to differentiate themselves from the Japanese forms.

The majority of these schools were teaching what are known as the "Pyung Ahn" forms (called *Pinan* or *Heian* in Japanese Karate schools) and other forms taken directly from Shotokan Karate systems.

In the late 1950's there were 2 different sets of forms created (to replace these Japanese forms), for use in these *Korean Karate* schools.

These were the ITF forms (also known as Chong Hon Tuls/Hyung, created by General Choi Hong Hi), all named after famous Korean heroes, such as Do-San and Yool Gok, two very famous men in Korean history; and *another* set of forms known as Palgwe (created just a bit earlier than the Chong Hon forms, but shunned by General Choi Hong Hi because they looked too much like Japanese Shotokan forms, so he created his Chong Han forms to be used in their place.)

Then, in 1967 the Koreans made the decision to create patterns that were *purely* Korean creations and named them Tae Geuk. The Korean masters decided to create simple forms that used "walking stances," with the theory that we fight standing more upright than we do in deep stances. I say, tell that to a wrestler.

The business-side of martial arts also came into play, as well as the need to quickly train military men, so the simplistic nature of the Tae Geuk forms and the walking stances allowed the forms to be quickly taught to the masses and was one of the reasons for Tae Kwon Do's rapid and growth all over the world.

The Tae Geuk forms are the standard WTF (World Tae Kwon Do Federation, which is the style that is associated with the *Olympic Sport*) forms that were adopted to replace the former Pyung Ahn (and other Japanese forms) that were being taught in the majority of these Korean Karate schools.

One of these factions (one of the original 5 "Kwans" of Korean Karate) known as "Mu Duk Kwan" adopted the name "Tang Soo Do" (formerly called "Soo Bahk Do" and recently revived as a name for the art) to describe their art, and this particular faction kept their Japanese (and Chinese) roots. Many of these schools have remained unchanged to this very day.

One look at any world map and it is clear that Korea is located right between northern China and Japan.

This makes it only natural to have influence from both countries.

The art of Tang Soo Do has strong influences from both Northern long fist Kung Fu and from Japanese Shotokan Karate, although the Tang Soo Do practitioners don't typically perform with the smoothness of Chinese movment. Their Chinese forms are basically performed just like their Japanese forms, and I suspect that this is part of what makes Korean Tang Soo Do/Soo Bahk Do (also known as Kong Soo Do in its infancy) unique from its Japanese counterpart of Shotokan Karate.

The *traditional* art of Tae Kwon Do (oftentimes linked with the ITF or International Tae Kwon Do Federation), created by General Choi Hong Hi in 1966, was obviously equally influenced, and often includes the art of Hapkido in its self-defense repertoire.

Even the more modern *sport* style of Tae Kwon Do has evolved since the mid 1980's and has been heavily influenced by the art of Wushu, in its kicking prowess.

Prior to the mid to late 1980's the multiple kicks of Tae Kwon Do, as we know them today, did not exist.

The Koreans have taken kicking to an entirely new level by refining their kicks into, arguably, the most devastating kicks of any single martial art.

All this being said, Chinese Kung Fu, and more specifically, the system taught throughout Korea should be of great interest to any practitioner of Korean martial arts such as Tae

Kwon Do, Tang Soo Do, Hapkido, Soo Bahk Do, Kuk Sool, Hwa Rang Do, etc....

Learning the secrets of this art can help bridge the gap between the original roots of the art that they currently practice and the original Chinese systems that they came from.

Chapter Fourteen

So Chu Kwon (Xiao Zi Quan)
(소축권) 小 縮 拳)

The first of the 4 core forms taught in most Korean Kung Fu systems is So Chu Kwon, Small Reducing Fist, which refers to the principle of developing power with short-range movements. The form teaches the practitioner how to develop power in the danjun (dantien, in Chinese) for creating explosive power in one's basic blocks and strikes. While it is a very simple form, it contains many important principles and techniques used in the advanced and black belt-level forms that are practiced in our system. It is primarily a Long Fist form. The form has 3 sections. Each time a direction is changed, the next section begins. There are a few different versions of this form floating around, one of which is a bit longer than others. I'm not sure if this longer version is an original version or if someone added to the form to make it more interesting. I have only ran across the longer version on a couple of occasions. The majority of the Sip Pal Gi systems that I've seen use the shorter pattern as is illustrated here.

---

*It should be noted that this book was not intended as a teaching tool. The forms contained in this book are more for reference and for the reader to get a basic understanding of how the forms look. Therefore, I will keep the descriptions of each movement as brief and simple as possible.

In order to fully understand and learn the forms, video needs to be seen. Videos of each of these forms are available at www.LTKFA.com. Of course, the very best way to learn these forms is through a qualified instructor that understands the basics used in the forms, and their associated self-defense applications.

Korean Kung Fu: The Chinese Connection

So Chu Kwon

1. ATTENTION

2. BOW/SALUTE

3. READY

4. LEFT PALM OUT TO SIDE

5. LEFT PALM BLOCK

6. CONTINUE ACROSS BODY

7. BRING TO RIGHT WAIST

8. DOUBLE SPEARS

9. DOUBLE MANTIS HOOKS

Chapter 14. SO CHU KWON

10. DOUBLE SPEARS RISING

11. TURN HANDS OVER

12. SEPARATE PALMS

13. BRING FISTS TO WAIST

14. STEP LEFT TO HORSE STANCE AND RAISE PALMS

15. PRESS PALMS DOWNWARD

16. SLIDE RIGHT FOOT TO LEFT DOUBLE SPEARS CLOSED

17. SLIDE TO LEFT (HORSE STANCE) SLAP INNER THIGHS AND LIFT ELBOWS

18. SHIFT TO LEFT MOUNTAIN STANCE RIGHT INNER FOREARM BLOCK

Korean Kung Fu: The Chinese Connection

19. SHIFT TO MANTIS STANCE
BRING LEFT ARM OVER HEAD

20. RIGHT HAMMER FIST

21. RAISE UP TO MOUNTAIN STANCE
KNIFE HANDS, PALMS OUT

22. TURN OVER (CAT STANCE)

23. DRAG FRONT LEG IN TO CLOSED
CAT STANCE, RAISE ARMS

24. DOUBLE SWEEPING BLOCK
TO REAR

25. SLIDE RIGHT LEG OUT TO SMALL
MOUNTAIN STANCE, BACK FIST

26. RAISE UP TO CAT STANCE
RIGHT UPPER BLOCK

27. LEFT UPPER BLOCK
FROM SAME STANCE

Chapter 14. SO CHU KWON

28. LIFT RIGHT KNEE TO CRANE STANCE, RIGHT FIST DROPS BACK

29. STEP DOWN INTO HORSE STANCE RIGHT UPPER CUT

30. LIFT LEFT KNEE INTO CRANE STANCE, GRAB WITH BOTH ARMS

31. PULL LEFT LEG BACK INTO HORSE STANCE, AND PULL ARMS TO WAIST

32. SHIFT TO MOUNTAIN STANCE LEFT BACKHAND STRIKE

33. STEP FORWARD TO RIGHT MOUNTAIN STANCE, RIGHT ELBOW

34. FROM SAME POSITION, RELEASE ELBOW, STRIKE INTO BACK/KNIFE HAND

35. PULL RIGHT FOOT BACK INTO CAT STANCE, ARMS OPEN TO SIDES

36. SLIDE FRONT FOOT BACK INTO MOUNTAIN STANCE, RIGHT FOREARM STRIKE

Korean Kung Fu: The Chinese Connection

37. STEP BEHIND WITH RIGHT FOOT
DROP ARMS TO LEFT WAIST

38. TURN TO REAR AND
HAMMER FIST STRIKE

39. LEAN BACK ON LEFT LEG

40. FROM LEAN BACK STANCE
BRING ARMS TO LEFT WAIST

41. SPRING FORWARD INTO HORSE
RIGHT UPPER BLOCK, LEFT ELBOW

42. SHIFT TO LEFT MOUNTAIN
STANCE
LEFT KNIFE-HAND BLOCK

43. FROM SAME POSITION
RIGHT PUNCH

44. LEAN BACK TO MANTIS STANCE
DRAG ARM TO REAR

45. SHIFT TO CRANE STANCE
LEFT HAMMER FIST, RIGHT FIST

Chapter 14. SO CHU KWON

46. STEP DOWN TO REAR RIGHT HAMMER FIST

47. STEP FORWARD RIGHT HAMMER FIST

48. FROM SAME POSITION RIGHT HAMMER FIST (DEEPER)

49. LEAN BACK CROSSING WEDGE BLOCK

50. WEDGE BLOCK AND SEPARATE ARMS

51. DOUBLE SPEARS MOUNTAIN STANCE

52. SKIP UP WHILE SEPARATING ARMS

53. SKIP UP TO CRANE STANCE PALMS TO WAIST

54. FROM SAME POSITION LOOK RIGHT

Korean Kung Fu: The Chinese Connection

55. STEP DOWN INTO MOUNTAIN STANCE, DOUBLE PALM STRIKE

56. STEP FORWARD TO RIGHT MOUNTAIN STANCE, UPPER CUT

57. SHIFT TO REAR, MOUNTAIN STANCE, LEFT KNIFE-HAND BLOCK

58. FROM SAME POSITION RIGHT PUNCH

59. SLIDE LEFT FOOT TO CENTER LEFT KNIFE-HAND STRIKE DOWN

60. RAISE PALMS SHIFTING TO ATTENTION STANCE

61. SLAP THIGHS WITH BACKS OF HANDS

62. CONTINUE CIRCLING HANDS UP AFTER STRIKING THIGHS

63. BRING FISTS DOWN NEAR DAN JUN (SETTLE THE KI)

64. BOW/SALUTE

Self Defense Applications of So Chu Kwon

Every martial arts form has associated self-defense techniques that hold the keys to understanding what each movement means. Self-defense applications are the subject of endless debates in the martial arts community and it should be noted that the following pictures and descriptions of how the techniques from the form So Chu Kwon are to be used are only a simplistic depiction of the technique's usage in real fighting.

That being said, I have put the pictures and descriptions together in a simple, orderly, flowing pattern that makes it easy to see where at in the form these techniques are drawn from.

It is important to note that I am only showing the "basic" applications of the techniques and that each technique generally has multiple applications.

For the reader who may look at the techniques and dismiss some of them as unusable, it is important to keep in mind that simply because a technique is taught does not mean that it will work in every situation, everytime, but <u>will</u> work under the right circumstances; and that goes for virtually any technique taught in any martial art.

Whether a technique works or not depends on several factors, including (but not limited to) timing, distance, size and shape of opponent, condition of ground surface, opponent's mental state, your mental state, condition of your body, condition of opponent's body, your understanding of the technique, how long you have trained using such a technique, etc., etc., etc…

For example, a basic throw used in Judo may work very well for a Judo player, but may completely fail if attempted by a person only trained in a striking art, who doesn't practice throwing their opponent on a regular basis.

Additionally, in Kung Fu the same technique that can be used to block a punch can also be used against a grab of some type.

For this self-defense application series, we are going to assume that we are dealing with two attackers and that one is in front of us and one is behind us.

The scenario might even be that we begin dealing with a single attacker and then a second attacker sees that his friend is fighting and comes to his aid, which would then account for only dealing with the second attacker at specific intervals. We can also view the turns as changes in direction during an altercation with a single opponent, or simply as a completely separate entity from the next technique.

We could literally fill an entire volume with all of the "what-ifs" of each technique. Rather than go that route, we will keep things straight forward, simple and stream-lined to give the reader a decent starting point for learning to decipher the self-defense applications of the form. After seeing the applications from So Chu Kwon you will have a general understanding of some of the basic applications for some of the movements from the other forms shown in this book. There is not enough room here to include the applications of the other forms. These applications can be seen on the DVD's that have been created for the other forms.

Chapter 14. SO CHU KWON

Technique #1

Opening Moves of Form

1. LEFT PALM BLOCK TO RIGHT PUNCH

2. CIRCLE PUNCH OUT OF THE WAY, RIGHT SPEAR TO THROAT

Technique #2

1. ATTACKER CHOKES

2. DOUBLE SPEARS TO BREAK GRIP

3. GRAB WRISTS

4. PULL TO KNEE STRIKE

Technique #3

1. BLOCK ONCOMING KICK TO GROIN

2. JOINED SPEAR HAND STRIKE TO THROAT

151

Korean Kung Fu: The Chinese Connection

Technique #4

1. BEAR HUG FROM BEHIND DROP DOWN TO HORSE STANCE, LIFT ELBOWS TO BREAK GRIP

2. DROP AND TURN, HOOK RIGHT LEG WITH RIGHT HAND, PULL HIS ARM WITH LEFT HAND

3. LIFT HIM ONTO YOUR BACK (FIREMAN'S CARRY)

4. HOIST HIM UP AND THROW HIM OVER TO GROUND

Technique #5

1. ATTACKER KICKS TO BODY SLIDE BACK TO CAT STANCE, HOOK WITH LEFT HAND, STRIKE SHIN WITH RIGHT HAND

2. PULL HIM TOWARD YOU AND BACK FIST STRIKE TO MANDIBLE JOINT

Technique #4

1. AGAINST PUNCH TO FACE, RIGHT UPPER BLOCK

2. CLEAR THE PUNCH WITH SECOND UPPER BLOCK WITH LEFT HAND

3. CATCH HIS PUNCHING ARM WITH LEFT HAND AND PULL, UPPER CUT TO SOLAR PLEXUS

Chapter 14. SO CHU KWON

Technique #5

1. AGAINST HAYMAKER PUNCH, CATCH PUNCH WITH LEFT HAND, GRAB UNDER ELBOW WITH RIGHT HAND, LIFT LEFT KNEE TO PULL BACKWARDS

2. PULL BACKWARD AND THROW OPPONENT OFF BALANCE TO THE REAR

3. CONTINUE PULL WITH LEFT HAND TO KEEP HIS BALANCE OFF, STEP IN AND STRIKE TO HEAD WITH RIGHT ELBOW

4. AFTER ELBOW STRIKE TO LEFT SIDE OF HIS HEAD, OPEN HAND AND STRIKE ON RIGHT MANDIBLE JOINT WITH BACK HAND

5. PULL BACK WHILE STILL HOLDING HIS RIGHT WRIST

6. FINISH HIM WITH POWERFUL INNER FOREARM STRIKE TO NECK

Korean Kung Fu: The Chinese Connection

Technique #6

1. AGAINST ONCOMING ATTACK FROM REAR, STEP BACK AND PREPARE TO BLOCK PUNCH

2. TWIST BODY TO FACE ATTACKER AND EXECUTE A POWERFUL HAMMER FIST BLOCK/STRIKE AT HIS ELBOW JOINT

3. STEP IN WITH LEFT LEG, GRAB HIS ARM AND PUSH UP WHILE EXECUTING LEFT ELBOW STRIKE TO RIBS (ELBOW STRIKE COMES FROM LEFT TO RIGHT)

4. BLOCK OR GRAB HIS RIGHT WRIST AND PREPARE TO PUNCH

5. OPPONENT ATTEMPTS TO PUNCH WITH FREE HAND, DEFENDER'S PUNCH GOES INSIDE OF ATTACKER'S PUNCH AND BLOCKS IT WHILE STRIKING

6. TWIST BODY AWAY WHILE CIRCLING ARMS BACK AND DOWN

7. LIFT RIGHT KNEE AS ARMS CONTINUE TO CIRCLE UP AND ACROSS, STRIKE HIM TO MANDIBLE JOINT WITH HAMMER FIST (TAN TUI #5/6)

Chapter 14. SO CHU KWON

Technique #7

1. OPPONENT ATTACKS FROM RIGHT SIDE, USE HAMMER FIST TO BLOCK/DESTROY HIS ARM
(TAN TUI #5)

2. STEP FORWARD AS HE PUNCHES WITH OTHER ARM, EXECUTE A SECOND HAMMER FIST STRIKE TO DESTROY HIS OTHER ARM

3. QUICKLY EXECUTE A THIRD HAMMER FIST STRIKE TO COLLAR BONE TO FINISH

Technique #8

1. OPPONENT ATTACKS WITH RIGHT HAYMAKER, LEAN BACK AND BLOCK PUNCH WITH LEFT OUTWARD FOREARM BLOCK

2. QUICKLY SKIP UP AND SWING ARMS IN WIDE CIRCLE

3. BRING HANDS TO WAIST

4. SHIFT WEIGHT TO LEFT LEG AND VIOLENTLY EXECUTE DOUBLE PALM STRIKE TO SOLAR PLEXUS

5. FULLY EXTEND AND KNOCK OPPONENT BACK

6. STEP THROUGH AND EXECUTE UPPER CUT

Technique #9

AGAINST RIGHT PUNCH TO HEAD
LEFT KNIFE HAND BLOCK, RIGHT PUNCH TO SOLAR PLEXUS

Technique #10

AGAINST LEFT PUNCH
RIGHT BACK OF HAND DEFLECT (OR PALM BLOCK), LEFT DOWNWARD KNIFE HAND (OR PALM) STRIKE TO FACE

Chapter Fifteen

Ag Ga Kwon/Yue Jia Quan
(악가권) 岳 家 拳

The second form in many Sip Pal Gi systems is known as Ag Ga Kwon, named after General Ag Be (Yue Fei in Chinese). It was created in his honor. Again, some systems use more of a praying mantis influence in the movements, while others have more of a pure long-fist feel to it. While it is the shortest form in our system, it contains many movements used in our advanced forms later in the system.

This form has a slightly different feel to it than So Chu Kwon. The movements flow easily from one technique to the next and, due to its short length, there are only two sections. The practitioner begins section one by moving to the left, then there is a turn-over technique which faces the practitioner in the other direction, and then the movements head back in the opposite direction so that the practitioner ends in the same spot that he started.

1. FEET TOGETHER, BOW
2. HANDS AT SIDES 
3. SLIDE HANDS UP SIDES

Korean Kung Fu: The Chinese Connection

4. DOUBLE SPEARS

5. RAISE PALMS OVER HEAD

6. SEPARATE PALMS

7. BRING FISTS TO WAIST

8. LOOK LEFT

9. STEP ACROSS INTO SCISSOR STANCE, LEFT PALM BLOCK

10. CHANGE TO MANTIS HOOK SAME POSITION

11. PULL MANTIS HOOK TO LEFT

12. LIFT LEFT KNEE

Chapter 15. AG GA KWON / YUE JIA QUAN

13. LEFT SIDE KICK

14. RE-CHAMBER LEFT KNEE TO CRANE STANCE, LEFT PALM BLOCK

15. STEP THROUGH TO RIGHT MOUNTAIN STANCE, RIGHT PUNCH

16. RIGHT PALM BLOCK

17. LEFT PALM BLOCK, SWITCH TO SEVEN STAR STANCE

18. STRAIGHTEN RIGHT ARM OUT BEHIND

19. RIGHT INNER FOREARM STRIKE FROM SAME POSITION

20. STILL HOLDING WRIST ASSISTED LOW BLOCK

21. RIGHT HEEL KICK TO BLADDER

Korean Kung Fu: The Chinese Connection

22. WHILE RE-CHAMBERING KNEE REACH OUT WITH LEFT HAND

23. CIRCLE LEFT ARM DOWN AND BACK UP

24. LEFT MANTIS CATCH WHILE STOMPING WITH RIGHT LEG (CAT STANCE)

25. JUMP INTO AIR WHILE EXECUTING INNER FOREARM STRIKE

26. TRY TO GET BOTH FEET HIGH OFF GROUND WHILE STRIKING

27. LAND AND LOOK LEFT (TO SEE NEXT OPPONENT)

28. DRIVE RIGHT ELBOW TO RIGHT HORSE STANCE

29. LOOK LEFT AND DROP ARMS TO REAR

30. PICK UP RIGHT KNEE TO CRANE STANCE

Chapter 15. AG GA KWON/YUE JIA QUAN

31. LOOK OVER SHOULDER

32. TURN CLOCKWISE

33. CONTINUE TURNING (THIS IS A JUMP TURN)

34. LAND IN A CAT STANCE LEFT HAMMER FIST, RIGHT PULL

35. BRING ARMS DOWN TO RIGHT

36. TWIST INTO SCISSOR STANCE DOUBLE PALM DEFLECT

37. BRING RIGHT FOOT FORWARD TO FOOT HOOK, MANTIS HOOKS PULL TO RIGHT

38. LEAN FORWARD TO MOUNTAIN STANCE, LEFT MANTIS CATCH

39. RIGHT INNER FOREARM STRIKE

Korean Kung Fu: The Chinese Connection

40. ASSISTED LOW BLOCK INTO LEFT PALM (THUMBLESS GRIP)

41. LEAN BACK

42. SPRING FORWARD

43. RIGHT UPPER BLOCK

44. LEFT PUNCH AND LEFT KICK SIMULTANEOUSLY

45. RE-CHAMBER KICK, STOMP ONTO LEFT FOOT, LEFT MANTIS CATCH

46. STEP FORWARD TO MOUNTAIN STANCE RIGHT ELBOW STRIKE TO LEFT PALM

47. RIGHT FOOT RETRACTS TO CAT STANCE ARMS TO RIGHT WAIST

48. RIGHT FOOT STEPS BACK OUT RIGHT VERTICAL PUNCH, LEFT UPPER BLOCK

Chapter 15. AG GA KWON / YUE JIA QUAN

49. LEFT PRESSING BLOCK

50. LEFT FRONT SNAP KICK SKIPPING INTO RIGHT LEG KICK

51. FROM LEFT LEG KICK SKIP INTO RIGHT FRONT SNAP KICK UPPER PUNCH (TAN TUI #8)

52. WHILE RE-CHAMBERING RIGHT KICK LEFT UPPER BLOCK (OPEN HAND)

53. RIGHT FOOT STEPS DOWN INTO HORSE STANCE, SIDE PUNCH AS LEFT HAND CLOSES TO WAIST

54. PULL LEFT FOOT TO RIGHT FISTS TO WAIST

55. BOW/SALUTE

Chapter Sixteen

Mei Hwa Kwon/Mei Hua Quan

(매화권)梅 花 拳

Mei Hwa Kwon (Plum Blossom Fist) is a very popular and easily recognizable form in nearly all Sip Pal Gi systems. There is also a set of 3 particular forms called Mei Hwa Kwon in the 7-Star Praying Mantis system that are different from the version shown in this book. These 3 praying mantis forms are called, Mei Hwa Soo Kwon (Mei Hua Shou Quan, in Chinese, Plum Blossom Hand Boxing), Mei Hwa Ro Kwon (Mei Hua Lo/Lu Quan, in Chinese, Plum Blossom Falling Boxing) and Mei Hwa Kwon (Mei Hua Quan, In Chinese, Plum Blossom Boxing/Fist), and are taught in that particular order and always as a complete set.

There are also several Shaolin versions that look different from the Sip Pal Gi version taught in our system, but a few of the versions have the same dropping scissor kick in them. (see pic 64)

This form is the sister form to Kum Gang Kwon (Jin Gang Quan) and has many similarities to it.

While Mei Hwa Kwon is typically taught *before* Kum Gang Kwon, Mei Hwa Kwon is a technically superior form to Kum Gang Kwon, however, Kum Gang Kwon is considered a higher level form due to the internal training aspects introduced in it.

Mei Hwa Kwon has a good blend of long fist and mantis and borrows techniques from both So Chu Kwon and Ag Ga

Kwon. The form So Ho Yun Kwon uses several techniques borrowed from this form. There are many excellent self-defense applications in this form. The form gets its name from the way it was constructed, in reference to the many opening and closing motions throughout the form, and one motion in particular, where the palms are pressed out to the sides while performing a high kick to the opponent's throat area (or solar plexus, or groin area.) See images 41-43.

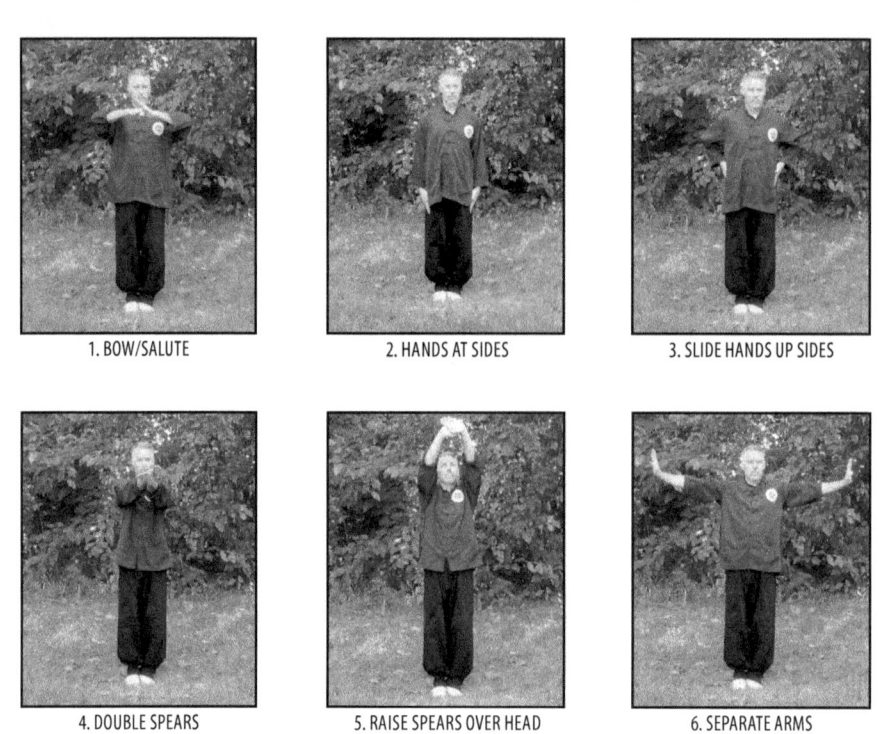

1. BOW/SALUTE

2. HANDS AT SIDES

3. SLIDE HANDS UP SIDES

4. DOUBLE SPEARS

5. RAISE SPEARS OVER HEAD

6. SEPARATE ARMS

Chapter 16. MEI HWA KWON

7. CLOSE FISTS

8. BRING FISTS TO WAIST

9. LOOK LEFT

10. LEFT HAND ACROSS BODY

11. LEFT BACK HAND STRIKE

12. RIGHT ELBOW INTO LEFT HAND

13. OPEN ARMS AND PREPARE TO KICK WITH RIGHT LEG

14. OUTSIDE CRESCENT KICK (LEFT TO RIGHT) WITH RIGHT LEG

15. RE-CHAMBER RIGHT LEG

Korean Kung Fu: The Chinese Connection

16. STEP DOWN, RIGHT PUNCH

17. STEP FORWARD, LEFT PUNCH

18. STEP FORWARD, LEFT UPPER BLOCK

19. CIRCLE LEFT ARM DOWN PAST WAIST, RIGHT ARM CIRCLE UP

20. EXTEND LEFT PALM

21. RIGHT LOW BLOCK, STRIKING LEFT PALM

22. SHIFT TO MOUNTAIN STANCE

23. PREPARE FOR RIGHT INNER-FOREARM STRIKE

24. RIGHT FOREARM STRIKE AGAINST LEFT PALM (THUMBLESS GRIP)

Chapter 16. MEI HWA KWON

25. LEAN BACK ONTO LEFT FOOT

26. SPRING FORWARD, RIGHT BLOCK

27. LEFT PUNCH

28. RIGHT PUNCH

29. LEFT PUNCH

30. LEAN BACK, PREPARE BLOCK

31. LEFT KNIFE HAND BLOCK

32. RIGHT PUNCH

33. RIGHT FOOT STEP FORWARD TO SCISSOR STANCE, ARMS CIRCLE OVER HEAD

Korean Kung Fu: The Chinese Connection

34. STEP FORWARD TO MANTIS STANCE SWING ARMS TO REAR (TIGER CLAWS)

35. SHIFT TO MOUNTAIN STANCE TIGER CLAW BLOCK WITH LEFT, TIGER STRIKE TO GROIN

36. TURN TO REAR RIGHT KNIFE HAND BLOCK

37. LEFT PUNCH

38. STEP FORWARD, PALMS DROP

39. HIGH SCISSOR STANCE, PREP SPEARS

40. DOUBLE SPEARS (CROSSED)

41. SEPARATE PALMS OUTWARD

42. PICK UP RIGHT KNEE

Chapter 16. MEI HWA KWON

43. HIGH HEEL KICK TO CHIN MEI HWA TECHNIQUE

44. RE-CHAMBER LEG, PALMS BLOCK

45. STEP DOWN TO HIGH SCISSOR STANCE, PALMS DEFLECT TO RIGHT

46. PULL FISTS TO WAIST (CUP AND SAUCER)

47. U-PUNCH

48. BRING RIGHT LEG UP TO CRANE, RIGHT FIST UP, LEFT FIST DOWN

49. RIGHT FIST SHOOTS DOWN, LEFT FIST SHOOTS UP

50. LEFT PRESSING BLOCK

51. STEP DOWN TO SMALL MOUNTAIN STANCE, PREP RIGHT HAND

Korean Kung Fu: The Chinese Connection

52. RIGHT DOWNWARD BACK FIST

53. TURN RIGHT FIST OVER AND GRAB

54. PULL RIGHT FIST BACK, LEFT HAND STRIKES NECK (PULL THE BOW) CRANE STANCE

55. RIGHT FIST COMES TO WAIST

56. RIGHT VERTICAL PUNCH MOUNTAIN STANCE

57. RIGHT FIST OPENS TO KNIFE HAND

58. TURN TO REAR, RIGHT BLOCK

59. LEFT PUNCH

60. ARMS SWING ACROSS BODY CLOCKWISE

Chapter 16. MEI HWA KWON

61. SHIFT TO REAR

62. MOVE LEFT FOOT UNTIL PARALLEL

63. SHOOT LEFT LEG BEHIND RIGHT LEG

64. DROP AND KICK WITH LEFT LEG SCISSOR KICK

65. SWITCH AND KICK WITH RIGHT LEG

66. CLOSE UP STANCE GET UP TO FEET

67. LEAVE ARMS TO LEFT SIDE

68. SPRING UPWARD AND BACK

69. TURN AND LAND, BACK FIST

Korean Kung Fu: The Chinese Connection

70. TURN TO REAR, LEFT BLOCK

71. RIGHT PUNCH

72. SKIP FORWARD

73. KNIFE HAND BLOCK AGAIN

74. RIGHT PUNCH

75. TURN TO REAR, LEFT PALM BLOCK

76. RIGHT HAMMER FIST

77. STEP ACROSS WITH LEFT FOOT, HIGH SCISSOR STANCE

78. RIGHT UPPER BLOCK

Chapter 16. MEI HWA KWON

79. DROP RIGHT ARM

80. RIGHT CRANE STANCE
RIGHT ARM COMES UPWARD

81. RIGHT ARM QUICKLY BENDS
TOWARDS YOU, LEFT ARMS
QUICKLY SHOOTS AWAY FROM
YOU (ARM BREAK)

82. STOMP ON RIGHT FOOT
CRANE STANCE, RIGHT MANTIS
CATCH (TAN TUI #12)

83. SPRING FORWARD, LEFT INNER
FOREARM STRIKE
(MOUNTAIN STANCE)

84. TWIST INTO SCISSOR STANCE
PALMS BLOCK TO LEFT

85. FISTS PULL TO RIGHT
RIGHT FOOT HOOK (TRIP)

86. WEIGHT ON RIGHT LEG AND
QUICKLY SKIP FORWARD, ARMS UP
AND TO OTHER SIDE

87. LEFT FOOT HOOK, MANTIS HOOKS
TO LEFT (TRIPPING OPPONENT)

88. QUICKLY SHOOT ARMS TO LEFT
WIND-UP MOTION

89. LOW SPIN KICK
360 DEGREE

90. CONTINUE TURNING
WEIGHT ON BALL OF LEFT FOOT

91. CONTINUE TURNING

92. FINISH IN MOUNTAIN STANCE
LEFT INWARD FOREARM BLOCK

93. TURN BLOCK OVER TO FIST
PREPARE RIGHT ARM OVER HEAD

94. RIGHT INWARD FOREARM BLOCK

95. RAISE RIGHT KNEE

96. RIGHT HEEL KICK TO BLADDER

Chapter 16. MEI HWA KWON

97. RE-CHAMBER LEG, LEFT ARM PREPARES OVERHEAD

98. STEP DOWN TO MOUNTAIN STANCE LEFT INWARD FOREARM BLOCK

99. RAISE LEFT KNEE

100. LEFT HEEL KICK

101. RE-CHAMBER LEG CRANE STANCE

102. STOMP AND SWITCH FEET LEFT MANTIS CATCH

103. DROP RIGHT FIST BACK AND DOWN

104. CONTINUE RIGHT ARM OVERHEAD

105. OPEN LEFT PALM

106. QUICKLY SWITCH FEET AGAIN

107. DOWNWARD CHOPPING STRIKE

108. STEP BACK INTO MOUNTAIN STANCE WHILE STRIKING DOWNWARD

109. COMPLETE THE STRIKE

110. LEAN BACK TO CAT STANCE RIGHT UPPER BLOCK

111. FROM SAME POSITION LEFT UPPER BLOCK

112. STEP FORWARD WITH RIGHT FOOT TO MOUNTAIN STANCE, RIGHT PUNCH

113. FROM SAME POSITION LEFT PUNCH

114. FROM SAME POSITION RIGHT PUNCH

Chapter 16. MEI HWA KWON

115. DOUBLE SPEAR LOW

116. CIRCLE ARMS OVERHEAD

117. BRING FISTS TO WAIST

118. BOW/SALUTE

119. FACE FRONT, BOW/SALUTE

Chapter Seventeen

Kum Gang Kwon/Jin Gang Quan
(금강권)金剛拳

Kum Gang Kwon (Golden Fist) is the fourth of the 4 primary forms taught in majority of Sip Pal Gi systems around the world. I have yet to come across a Kung Fu school that teaches a similar system that does not teach this form (or the other 3 aforementioned forms for that matter).

This form is the sister form to Mei Hwa Kwon and features many of the same techniques and sequences. The form has a strong focus on power, and showcases this with movements that require additional power to perform *properly* to bring out the essence of it.

This form begins with a slightly different opening sequence than the other 3 forms in that it begins with a simple danjun breathing exercise used to generate Ki power. This particular form contains several Kum Na (Chin' Na) techniques that are very effective and painful.

Since this form begins with an introduction to Ki (Chi) breathing, which is part of our internal training, it is considered a higher-level form than Mei Hwa Kwon, even though the techniques used in this form are slightly easier to perform than those found in Mei Hwa Kwon.

There is also a modern Tae Kwon Do form that goes by Kumgang, but the Tae Kwon Do form has no relationship to the Kung Fu form, other than its name. Typically, the Tae Kwon Do version is written with no spaces, "Kumgang" while the Kung Fu version is written with spaces, "Kum Gang" and includes "Kwon" at the end to denote its Chinese heritage—Chinese forms usually have Quan/Chuan at the end, which means "boxing" or "fist" to denote a particular style of Kung Fu (similar to how other Korean styles use the term "hyung" at the end, such as in "Pyung Ahn Yi Dan Hyung").

1. FEET TOGETHER

2. BOW/SALUTE

3. FISTS AT WAIST

4. SLIDE HANDS UP

5. BEND FORWARD AT WAIST, SLIDE HANDS DOWN LEGS, KNEES LOCKED OUT

6. TURN PALMS UP

7. BRING HANDS UP

8. BRING HANDS OVER HEAD

9. TILT FINGERS DOWN

Chapter 17. KUM GANG KWON

10. REPEAT AGAIN
HANDS DOWN LEGS

11. TURN PALMS UP

12. BRING HANDS UP

13. BRING FISTS TO WAIST

14. LEFT PALM BLOCK
RIGHT MANTIS HOOK TO REAR

15. STEP FORWARD TO SMALL
MOUNTAIN STANCE, STRIKE LEFT
PALM WITH BACK OF MANTIS HAND

16. WHILE STILL HOLDING
RIGHT HAND, OPEN RIGHT HAND
(SAME POSITION)

17. TWIST RIGHT HAND OVER TO
PALM UP (FROM SAME POSITION)

18. GRAB WITH RIGHT HAND
LEFT HAND REMAINS ON TOP

183

19. STEP ACROSS TO
SCISSOR STANCE
RIGHT HAND PULLS TO WAIST
LEFT HAND PRESSES DOWNWARD

20. STEP FORWARD TO
MOUNTAIN STANCE
EXTEND RIGHT ARM TO REAR

21. FROM SAME POSITION
SWING RIGHT ARM UP AND STRIKE
LEFT PALM

22. TWIST INTO HIGH
SCISSOR STANCE
PALMS BLOCK TO LEFT

23. BRING RIGHT FOOT FORWARD
SHARPLY (FOOT HOOK)
PULL FISTS TOWARD RIGHT (TRIP)

24. BRING LEFT LEG BEHIND
(COUNTERCLOCKWISE)

25. LEFT KNIFE HAND BLOCK

26. RIGHT PUNCH

27. OPEN RIGHT PALM
BRING LEFT PALM AGAINST RIGHT
FOREARM

Chapter 17. KUM GANG KWON

28. PULL RIGHT FIST BACK NEAR EAR
LEFT KNIFE HAND STRIKE
(PULL THE BOW)

29. LAND IN HORSE STANCE
BRING RIGHT ARM OVER HEAD
LEFT PALM EXTENDED (AS TARGET)

30. RIGHT LOW BLOCK STRIKES
LEFT PALM
(ARM BREAK)

31. SHIFT TO MOUNTAIN STANCE
LEFT ARM EXTENDED TO REAR

32. LEFT INNER FOREARM STRIKE
TO RIGHT PALM
(PALM SIMULATES NECK
OF OPPONENT)

33. TURN TO REAR
LEFT KNIFE HAND BLOCK

34. RIGHT PUNCH
(FROM SAME POSITION)

35. LEFT PUNCH
(FROM SAME POSITION)

36. RIGHT PUNCH
(FROM SAME POSITION)

Korean Kung Fu: The Chinese Connection

**37. LEAN BACK
LEFT UPWARD PRESSING BLOCK**

38. CATCH ARM WITH LEFT MANTIS HOOK, STEP FORWARD TO HORSE STANCE, RIGHT ELBOW STRIKE TO RIBS

**39. LEAN BACK
CATCH OPPONENT'S ARM WITH RIGHT MANTIS HOOK**

**40. STEP FORWARD TO HORSE STANCE
LEFT ELBOW TO RIBS**

41. SLAP BACK OF LEFT HAND AGAINST LEFT INNER THIGH

42. BRING HAND UP TO PALM DEFLECT AS RIGHT LEG COMES FORWARD

43. STEP FORWARD TO MOUNTAIN STANCE, RIGHT VERTICAL PUNCH LEFT HAND PROTECTS RIBS

44. SHIFT FORWARD LEG BACK TO CAT STANCE, RAISE ARMS UPWARD

45. SLAP RIGHT THIGH WITH BACKS OF BOTH HANDS

Chapter 17. KUM GANG KWON

46. AFTER SLAPPING THIGHS RAISE HANDS OVER HEAD AGAIN (PALMS DOWN)

47. BLOCK DOWNWARD WITH BOTH PALMS, RIGHT PALM SLIGHTLY FURTHER OUT IN FRONT (BLOCKING KICK)

48. TWIST INTO SCISSOR STANCE DOUBLE PALM DEFLECT TO LEFT

49. DOUBLE MANTIS HOOKS (GRABBING OPPONENT'S ARM)

50. SIDE KICK

51. RE-CHAMBER FROM KICK

52. SHIFT TO CRANE STANCE RIGHT ARM BENT, LEFT ARM EXTENDED

53. STEP DOWN TO MOUNTAIN STANCE RIGHT HAMMER FIST (FROM LEFT EAR)

54. STEP FORWARD TO MOUNTAIN STANCE, PULL WITH RIGHT FIST LEFT OUTER FOREARM STRIKE

Korean Kung Fu: The Chinese Connection

55. SWING RIGHT LEG OUT (PREPARE TO SWEEP OPPONENT) LEFT ARM GRABBING ARM

56. QUICKLY PULL LEFT ARM NEAR EAR (REPRESENTS OPPONENT'S LIMB OR SLEEVE), RIGHT FOOT SWEEPS BACK

57. QUICKLY BRING RIGHT FOOT UP AND STOMP DOWN, PREPARE FOR LOW HAMMER FIST STRIKE TO REAR

58. SHIFT TO CLOSED CAT STANCE STRIKE TO GROIN WITH LOW HAMMER FIST WITH LEFT FIST

59. RAISE UP TO CRANE STANCE (TUCK RIGHT KNEE), EXECUTE RIGHT INNER FOREARM STRIKE

60. AFTER STRIKE, CONTINUE ARMS ACROSS BODY TO REAR ON LEFT SIDE (SLIGHT ANGLE TO CRANE STANCE)

61. STEP DOWN INTO MOUNTAIN STANCE, RIGHT HAMMER FIST STRIKE EXTEND LEFT ARM TO REAR

62. STEP FORWARD TO MOUNTAIN STANCE, PULL RIGHT HAND BACK AND EXECUTE LEFT OUTER FOREARM STRIKE

63. WITH FISTS IN SAME POSITION QUICKLY SKIP FORWARD

Chapter 17. KUM GANG KWON

64. LAND IN SAME POSITION AS #62

65. FROM SAME POSITION QUICK, SHORT LEFT JAB

66. QUICK SHORT RIGHT JAB

67. BRING RIGHT KNEE UP TO CRANE STANCE, TWIST PALMS UPWARD (GRABBING OPPONENT'S LIMB)

68. PULL RIGHT LEG BACK AND DOWN TO HORSE STANCE, PULL FISTS TO RIGHT WAIST (SAME TIME AS LEG LANDS)

69. LOOK RIGHT

70. STEP ACROSS WITH LEFT LEG (IN FRONT) TO SCISSOR STANCE SEPARATE ARMS TO PREPARE FOR BLOCK

71. RIGHT UPPER BLOCK (OPEN HAND) LEFT GUARDING POSITION NEAR FACE

72. BLOCK AND CATCH WITH MANTIS HOOKS, PULL TO LEFT SIDE OF BODY

Korean Kung Fu: The Chinese Connection

73. RIGHT SIDE KICK

74. RE-CHAMBER KICK BRINGS ARMS ACROSS BODY TO LEFT SIDE

75. SHIFT TO CRANE STANCE RIGHT ARM BENT, LEFT ARM EXTENDED

76. STEP FORWARD TO MOUNTAIN STANCE, RIGHT HAMMER FIST FROM LEFT EAR AREA

77. STEP FORWARD TO MOUNTAIN STANCE, PULL WITH RIGHT FIST, LEFT OUTER FOREARM STRIKE TO CLAVICLE

78. LEFT PRESSING BLOCK (FROM SAME POSITION)

79. RIGHT TIGER'S MOUTH STRIKE (AKA "C-STRIKE")

80. SEPARATE PALMS

81. RIGHT OUTSIDE CRESCENT KICK (KICK BOTH PALMS WITH OUTSIDE OF RIGHT FOOT)

Chapter 17. KUM GANG KWON

82. RE-CHAMBER FROM KICK EXTEND RIGHT PALM TO REAR

83. TURN AND EXECUTE LEFT ELBOW INTO EXTENDED PALM

84. QUICKLY SHOOT LEFT PALM OUT AND PALM BLOCK AS RIGHT FIST DROPS UNDER

85. RIGHT DOWNWARD BACK FIST STRIKE

86. LEAN BACK TO LEFT LEG RIGHT PALM BLOCK/STRIKE

87. QUICKLY STOMP RIGHT FOOT AND SWITCH FEET TO LEFT FOOT HOOK, LEFT INNER FOREARM STRIKE

88. LEFT FOOT STEPS BEHIND PREPARE FOR LEFT KNIFE HAND BLOCK WITH TURN

89. TURN TO REAR LEFT KNIFE HAND BLOCK

90. FROM SAME POSITION RIGHT PUNCH

Korean Kung Fu: The Chinese Connection

91. SIMULTANEOUSLY PUNCH WITH LEFT HAND AND KICK WITH RIGHT FOOT

92. DURING THE RE-CHAMBER FROM THE KICK, LEFT UPPER BLOCK

93. STEP OUT TO HORSE STANCE AS LEFT ARM CIRCLES DOWN AND EXTENDS OUT

94. LOW BLOCK/LIMB BREAK

95. SLIDE RIGHT FOOT BACK INTO HIGH CAT STANCE, RIGHT UPPER BLOCK

96. FROM SAME POSITION LEFT UPPER BLOCK

97. SLIDE RIGHT FOOT OUT TO HORSE STANCE, SIDE PUNCH

98. SLIDE LEFT FOOT TO RIGHT FOOT FISTS AT WAIST

99. BOW/SALUTE

Chapter Eightteen

So Ho Yun Kwon/Xiao Hu Yan Quan

(소호연권)小 虎 燕 拳

So Ho Yun Kwon is probably the most revered form in all of Korean martial arts. Korean martial artists from all backgrounds have sought out proper instruction in this form and it continues to be taught in many Tang Soo Do, Tae Kwon Do, Kang Duk Won, and, of course, Korean Kung Fu schools around the world. It is a favorite among the majority of masters of the Korean Kung Fu systems, even though there are several higher-level forms that come after it.

This particular form can be seen in numerous Chinese systems as well; most notably (and not surprisingly) Northern Long Fist and Northern Praying Mantis systems. Each version looks a little different from the other, but there are specific core movements that are included in each of the various versions, and in the exact same order.

I have collected so many different video performances of this form that I have quite literally lost count. The Chinese name for this form is known as Shao Hu Yan Quan. Other spellings are Xiao Hu Yan Quan, and Hsiao Hu Yen Chuan. Typically, in Korean circles, the form is simply called, "So Ho Yun."

The English translations vary slightly from person to person; from Little Flying Tiger, to Little Tiger Playing by the Pond, to Little Tiger Swallow Fist, Small Tiger Goose Fist, or simply, Little Tiger.

According to a legend that was handed down, a martial arts practitioner was walking down a road somewhere in China and came across a beautifully painted mural of a large tiger with wings and was so inspired by the beauty of the mural that he created a form and called it, "Little Flying Tiger."

I obviously have nothing to back this up, other than word of mouth, as it was told to me by a few different masters. I have also been told that So Ho Yun was the first Praying Mantis form ever created, which would explain why it is seen in both Praying Mantis systems as well as in Long Fist systems, since Long Fist was created prior to Praying Mantis. Who knows? Could it be that the martial arts practitioner who saw the mural may have been Wang Lang himself?

Wang Lang was the man who created the Praying Mantis system, after watching a praying mantis fight other insects and creatures; and he took the concepts and created his art, which was recognized by the Shaolin Temple as being a *superior* art to Long Fist, as well as many other styles taught at the Temple, prior to the introduction of Praying Mantis by Wang Lang. Some sources suggest that this form comes from a Long Fist system called "Mizong Quan (Lost Track Boxing)."

It's unclear as to why the Korean version looks vastly different from most of the other versions that I have seen, but there is clearly a connection. The basics of So Ho Yun are simply parts of Tan Tui strung together, and there are elements taken from the forms Mei Hwa Kwon and Kum Gang Kwon represented in the form as well.

So Ho Yun is one of the longer forms in the system, and is considered by many to be the flagship form of the entire system.

Chapter 18. SO HO YUN KWON

In all of the Korean versions that I have seen and learned, there are some subtle differences, but, overall, the form is taught the same way across the board. The set of movements, known as the "signature movements" are what gives the form its unique *Korean-version* identity.

There are some variations on how the form begins and ends, but, nearly everything in between is pretty consistent from school to school.

The signature movements in the form begin with a double upper block into a right side punch from a horse stance (Tan Tui #10), followed by a crane stance and a straight left uppercut and a punch/block downward, from a crane stance, and a jumping hammer fist/back fist strike from a mountain stance. (Fig. 48-54)

It is a highly challenging form and will take your breath away after a single performance. The form should be performed at varying speeds throughout, with several pauses to accentuate the performance and bring out both the essences of the tiger and the swallow.

While there are no actual "tiger" claw movements (except one–see image 61), as one might see in Nam Kwon (Nan Quan style , in Chinese, which means Southern Fist), the name was given to the form to support the "essence" of the ferocity of the tiger and the gracefulness of a swallow (a small bird). Therefore, the form should be performed with small bursts of great energy and blended with subtle smooth, graceful elements, to really bring out the flavor of this form.

It is very powerful and very graceful at the same time. There are also two jumping kicks in the form, which lend themselves to the movements of a sparrow, while being ferocious like a tiger, and the eyes are fixated on the opponent in a way that teaches the practitioner to stare through the very soul of his opponent while also helping to bring out intensity and strong eye-contact. Regular practice of So Ho Yun will greatly enhance a practitioner's power, grace and rhythm.

The goal is to cover as much ground as possible with each movement and to finish precisely where it was started. This alone will tax the practitioner's legs and lungs greatly; it's more difficult than it sounds.

There is also a 2-person version of So Ho Yun that is practiced in some Praying Mantis systems. I have video of this form, which can help one to understand some of the possible applications of the techniques and is very interesting and beautiful to watch.

In order to properly learn So Ho Yun one must be taught by a qualified master in order to learn all of the intricacies of this form. There are several techniques taught in the form that are difficult, if not impossible to discover the self-defense applications of without being shown.

In our particular system, we have a 2nd version of So Ho Yun (So Ho Yun Yi Dan) that I have not seen anywhere else with the exception of one school in Korea. Consequently, my master trained with the same master as the Master of that school in Korea, so, it doesn't surprise me too much. I'm not certain as to when or who created it, and it has a lot of the same techniques as in So Ho Yun, but has some additional techniques, including low sweeps with the *left* leg as well as the right leg.

Chapter 18. SO HO YUN KWON

1. FISTS AT SIDES

2. BOW/SALUTE

3. FISTS AT SIDES

4. LEFT PALM BLOCK ACROSS BODY
CLOSED CAT STANCE

5. CONTINUE UNTIL HANDS ARE AT
RIGHT HIP, PALMS UP

6. LEFT FOOT STEPS FORWARD
DOUBLE SPEARS
MOUNTAIN STANCE

7. TURN SPEARS OVER

8. DOUBLE MANTIS HOOK TO REAR
SHIFT TO CAT STANCE

9. BRING RIGHT LEG FORWARD
FEET TOGETHER
DOUBLE SPEARS UPWARD

Korean Kung Fu: The Chinese Connection

10. DOUBLE SPEARS UPWARD CONTINUED

11. TURN PALMS OVER

12. SEPARATE HANDS

13. BRING FISTS TO WAIST

14. BEND KNEES AND PALM BLOCK TO LEFT

15. STEP OUT TO HORSE STANCE SIDE PUNCH

16. LEAN BACK, LEFT KNIFE HAND BLOCK AND STEP FORWARD

17. LAND IN ANOTHER HORSE STANCE SIDE PUNCH

18. SLIDE RIGHT FOOT TO LEFT FOOT AND RAISE RIGHT HAND OVER HEAD DROP LEFT HAND NEAR WAIST

Chapter 18. SO HO YUN KWON

19. QUICKLY BRING RIGHT KNEE UP TO CRANE STANCE, SHOOT LEFT FIST STRAIGHT UP, RIGHT FIST DOWN

20. JUMP AND TURN CLOCKWISE TO REAR, LEFT HAND PRESSING BLOCK

21. LAND IN MOUNTAIN STANCE RIGHT DOWNWARD BACK FIST STRIKE

22. TURN TO REAR LEFT KNIFE HAND BLOCK

23. RIGHT PUNCH

24. LEFT PUNCH, RIGHT KICK SIMULTANEOUSLY

25. RE-CHAMBER KICK LEFT OPEN-HANDED UPPER BLOCK RIGHT FIST DROPS BACK AND DOWN

26. LAND IN HORSE STANCE, RIGHT ARMS CONTINUES CIRCLING OVER HEAD, LOW BLOCK/LIMB BREAK

27. SLIDE FRONT LEG BACK INTO HIGH CAT STANCE, RIGHT ARM BLOCKS OUTWARD

Korean Kung Fu: The Chinese Connection

28. CONTINUE PULLING RIGHT BLOCK BACKWARD, LEFT HAND ASSISTS BLOCK

29. STEP OUT TO HORSE STANCE SIDE PUNCH

30. SHIFT TO MOUNTAIN STANCE, WIND ARMS UP FOR JUMP INSIDE CRESCENT KICK

31. PUT WEIGHT ON RIGHT LEG WHILE TURNING, LIFT LEFT LEG AND JUMP

32. WHILE IN AIR, EXECUTE INSIDE CRESCENT KICK TO LEFT PALM

33. RE-CHAMBER KICK AS YOU LAND ON LEFT FOOT

34. LEFT UPPER BLOCK CAT STANCE

35. STEP OUT TO HORSE STANCE SIDE PUNCH

36. SLIDE RIGHT LEG BACK UNTIL FEET ARE TOGETHER, RIGHT HAND EXTENDS UPWARD, LEFT HAND DOWNWARD

Chapter 18. SO HO YUN KWON

37. RIGHT KNEE UP (CRANE STANCE), SHOOT LEFT FIST STRAIGHT UP, SHOOT RIGHT FIST STRAIGHT DOWN

38. SPRING UPWARD TO REAR CLOCKWISE LEFT HAND PRESSING BLOCK

39. LAND IN MOUNTAIN STANCE, RIGHT DOWNWARD BACK FIST

40. TURN TO REAR LEFT KNIFE HAND BLOCK

41. RIGHT PUNCH

42. LEFT PUNCH FROM SAME POSITION

43. RIGHT PUNCH

44. SHIFT TO REAR RIGHT HAMMER FIST

45. SLIP LEFT HAND OUT AND ROTATE PALM, PULL RIGHT FIST TO WAIST

Korean Kung Fu: The Chinese Connection

46. PRESS LEFT HAND DOWN WHILE RAISING UP TO CRANE STANCE, RIGHT ARM SHOOTS STRAIGHT UP

47. PULL LEFT FIST TO WAIST, DROP TO HORSE STANCE, RIGHT ELBOW STRIKE

48. PULL RIGHT LEG BACK TO CAT STANCE, RIGHT UPPER BLOCK

49. FROM SAME POSITION LEFT UPPER BLOCK

50. STEP RIGHT LEG OUT TO HORSE STANCE, SIDE PUNCH

51. SLIDE RIGHT LEG BACK RAISE RIGHT HAND, DROP LEFT HAND TO SIDE

52. PICK UP RIGHT KNEE TO CRANE STANCE, SHOOT LEFT FIST STRAIGHT UP SHOOT RIGHT FIST STRAIGHT DOWN

53. JUMP AND TURN CLOCKWISE TO REAR, LEFT HAND PRESSING BLOCK

54. UPON LANDING FROM JUMPING TURN, RIGHT BACK FIST MOUNTAIN STANCE

Chapter 18. SO HO YUN KWON

55. TURN TO REAR LEFT KNIFE HAND BLOCK MOUNTAIN STANCE

56. FROM SAME POSITION RIGHT PALM STRIKE

57. FROM SAME POSITION LEFT PALM STRIKE

58. RIGHT KNEE FORWARD AND UP TO CRANE STANCE, RIGHT HAND OPEN UPPER BLOCK, LEFT HAND ASSISTS

59. FROM SAME POSITION LEFT KNIFE HAND STRIKE TO NECK

60. DRAW LEFT HAND BACK IN RIGHT HAND UPPER CUT TO SOLAR PLEXUS, HORSE STANCE

61. OPEN RIGHT FIST AND GRAB CLOTHING (OR FLESH)

62. LEFT PALM STRIKE TO SOLAR PLEXUS

63. SLAP BACKS OF HANDS AGAINST INNER THIGHS

Korean Kung Fu: The Chinese Connection

64. AFTER SLAPPING THIGHS CONTINUE RAISING HANDS UPWARD PALMS UP

65. CONTINUE RAISING HANDS OVER HEAD

66. DOUBLE PALM PRESS

67. QUICKLY STOMP ONTO RIGHT FOOT, SWING LEFT LEG AND ARM BACK
RIGHT ARM PRESSING BLOCK

68. STEP FORWARD TO MOUNTAIN STANCE, LEFT UPPER CUT

69. STEP BACK WITH LEFT LEG PREPARE TO BLOCK WITH RIGHT ARM

70. SHIFT TO PRAYING MANTIS STANCE WHILE BLOCKING WITH OUTER FOREARM
LEFT FIST BEHIND HEAD

71. SHIFT WEIGHT FORWARD TO MOUNTAIN STANCE
LEFT PRESSING BLOCK

72. FROM SAME POSITION RIGHT DOWNWARD BACK FIST

Chapter 18. SO HO YUN KWON

73. TURN TO REAR
LEFT KNIFE HAND BLOCK
MOUNTAIN STANCE

74. FROM SAME POSITION
RIGHT PUNCH

75. RIGHT FOOT SLIDES FORWARD
TO CAT STANCE
RIGHT HAND BLOCKS INWARD
TO LEFT

76. RIGHT SPEAR-HAND STRIKE

77. LEFT SPEAR-HAND STRIKE OVER
RIGHT PALM

78. LEFT ARM DROPS TO LEFT, RIGHT
ARM DROPS TO RIGHT. BOTH HANDS
BECOME MANTIS HOOKS

79. LEFT MANTIS HOOK RAISES TO
SHOULDER LEVEL, RIGHT MANTIS
HOOK RAISES TO UPPER
BLOCK LEVEL

80. LEFT ARM BLOCKS INWARD
RIGHT HAND BLOCKS OUTWARD
TO RIGHT

81. HANDS CONTINUE CIRCLING
UNTIL RIGHT HAND IS OVER HEAD
HIGH SCISSOR STANCE

Korean Kung Fu: The Chinese Connection

82. QUICKLY THROW LEFT LEG UP IN AIR AND JUMP, RIGHT LEG REMAINS STRAIGHT, RIGHT HAND OUT

83. RIGHT LEG SWINGS UP AS RIGHT PALM MEETS FOOT AT EYE LEVEL, FRONT SLAP KICK

84. AFTER STRIKING PALM, LAND ON LEFT FOOT

85. RE-CHAMBER RIGHT LEG ARMS CIRCLE OVERHEAD CLOCKWISE

86. QUICKLY STOMP ON RIGHT FOOT, LEFT FOOT HOOK, ARMS FINISH IN MANTIS HOOKS

87. TWIST BODY TO LEFT (SET UP FOR SWEEP)

88. DROP AND TURN PLACE PALMS ON GROUND EXTEND RIGHT LEG STRAIGHT

89. LOW SPINNING WHEEL KICK STAY ON BALL OF RIGHT FOOT LEFT FOOT BLADED

90. CONTINUE SPINNING KEEP RIGHT FOOT CONNECTED TO GROUND

Chapter 18. SO HO YUN KWON

91. FINISH SPIN AND SHIFT TO MOUNTAIN STANCE

92. RAISE BODY AND INNER FOREARM BLOCK WITH LEFT

93. QUICKLY STOMP RIGHT FOOT NEXT TO LEFT GRAB LEFT FIST WITH RIGHT HAND

94. SHOOT HANDS STRAIGHT UP LEFT CRANE STANCE

95. LOOK TO RIGHT HORSE STANCE

96. LEFT ELBOW RIGHT PALM PRESSES FIST FOR MORE POWERFUL STRIKE

97. PUT WEIGHT ONTO LEFT KNEE SHIFT AND TURN TO REAR GRAB OPPONENT

98. PULL OPPONENT IN LEFT CRANE STANCE (KNEE STRIKE)

99. DOUBLE PALM STRIKE LEFT BACK KICK SIMULTANEOUSLY

Korean Kung Fu: The Chinese Connection

100. DROP LEFT LEG IN FRONT OF RIGHT LEG (SCISSOR STANCE) LEFT PRESSING BLOCK

101. STEP FORWARD TO MOUNTAIN STANCE RIGHT DOWNWARD BACK FIST

102. SKIP FORWARD ONTO RIGHT LEG, LEFT ARM DROPS AND PREPARES TO BLOCK

103. SKIPPING CONTINUED LEFT KNIFE HAND BLOCK

104. FINISH SKIPPING IN MOUNTAIN STANCE

105. SHIFT TO HORSE STANCE SIDE PUNCH

106. SLIDE RIGHT LEG TO LEFT RIGHT HAND STRAIGHT UP, LEFT HAND STRAIGHT DOWN KNEES BENT

107. RIGHT KNEE LIFTS TO CRANE STANCE, RIGHT FIST SHOOTS DOWN LEFT FIST SHOOTS UP

108. JUMP AND TURN CLOCKWISE LEFT PRESSING BLOCK

208

Chapter 18. SO HO YUN KWON

109. RIGHT DOWNWARD BACK FIST MOUNTAIN STANCE

110. LEAN BACK TO LEFT MANTIS STANCE, LEFT UPPER BLOCK RIGHT INWARD FOREARM STRIKE

111. SHIFT WEIGHT TO RIGHT MANTIS STANCE, RIGHT UPPER BLOCK, LEFT INWARD FOREARM STRIKE

112. SHIFT WEIGHT TO LEFT LEG CAT STANCE, RIGHT ARM STRIKES INTO LEFT PALM (GRAB WRIST)

113. RIGHT KNEE LIFTS STILL HOLDING RIGHT WRIST WITH LEFT HAND

114. RIGHT INVERTED ROUNDHOUSE KICK (TWIST KICK)

115. DROP RIGHT LEG ACROSS BODY, STILL GRABBING RIGHT WRIST LOOK LEFT

116. LIFT LEFT KNEE STILL GRABBING RIGHT WRIST WITH LEFT HAND

117. LEFT INVERTED ROUNDHOUSE KICK (TWIST KICK) STILL HOLDING RIGHT WRIST

Korean Kung Fu: The Chinese Connection

118. STEP FORWARD TO MOUNTAIN STANCE, LEFT PRESSING BLOCK RIGHT HAND EXTENDS TO REAR

119. RIGHT UPPER CUT

120. TURN TO REAR, PREPARE FOR KNIFE HAND BLOCK

121. FROM SAME POSITION LEFT KNIFE HAND BLOCK

122. RIGHT PUNCH

123. LEFT ELBOW RAISES WHILE LEFT FOOT SLIDES FROM MOUNTAIN STANCE TO CAT STANCE

124. LEFT HAND COMES FORWARD AND DOWN TO KNIFE HAND BLOCK POSE, RIGHT HAND UNDER LEFT ELBOW

125. SLIDE LEFT FOOT FORWARD RAISE PALMS

126. SLAP THIGHS WITH BACKS OF HANDS

Chapter 18. SO HO YUN KWON

127. AFTER SLAPPING THIGHS CONTINUE RAISING ARMS OVER HEAD

128. BRING FISTS TO WAIST (SETTLE THE KI)

129. BOW/SALUTE

Chapter Nineteen

About My Teachers

As you have already learned from Chapter One, I have had many teachers. The majority of my teachers from 1983 to present have been of Korean decent. I have learned so much from so many different teachers, and each of them has provided a piece to the proverbial puzzle.

My first Korean teacher, as I mentioned was Grandmaster Young Pyo Choi. When I first met Grandmaster Choi, I was about 14 years old. I believe Grandmaster Choi was 35 years old when I first met him. He had just moved to Indianapolis in December of 1982 after spending approximately 10 years teaching with his brother, Grandmaster Joon Pyo Choi in Columbus, Ohio.

Grandmaster Choi moved to Indianapolis to branch out and develop his own system. He eventually coined his system, "Moo Jung Ryu," around the year 2000 or 2001, which translates into "The Righteous Way of Martial Arts."

He never told anyone the name of his original Kung Fu teacher(s) and said that he traveled to a "temple" to learn various types of martial arts where masters would share with one another. His brother (more on him in a moment) invited him to move to the United States and Grandmaster Young Choi (pronounced "Chay") was forced to make a decision; at that time he was a professional tennis champion in Korea, and a former drill sergeant in the Korean Rok Marines.

He was not sure about his future, but decided to bite the

proverbial bullet, and move to the United States with his brother to help him build their organization; known as the "Oriental Martial Arts College."

Grandmaster Young Pyo Choi and James Theros, 1999

When he came over, the brothers formed an alliance with Grandmaster Ki Whang Kim, (who was also known for his experience in Korean Kung Fu) and Grandmaster Byung Jik Ro. I can remember meeting Grandmaster Ki Whang Kim when I was just a beginner. He sat in on one or two of my first tests. We traveled to his tournament in the Washington D.C. area when I was a green belt and I competed at my first tournament at his event.

Chapter 19. ABOUT MY TEACHERS

Grandmaster
Ki Whang Kim

Founder of Song Moo Kwan,
Grandmaster Byung Jik Ro

There was always talk about both Grandmaster Ro and Grandmaster Kim. The system that we were told we were learning was called, Song Moo Kwan (The Pinetree School/System), which was one of the original 5 Kwans (there were eventually 9 Kwans altogether). It should also be noted that the creators of the original 5 Kwans were all friends and freely shared information back and forth with one another. Song Moo Kwan was the first of the Kwans established, and it was created by Grandmaster Byung Jik Ro.

Grandmaster Young Pyo Choi studied with both Grandmaster Ro and Grandmaster Kim, and had been learning his Kung Fu system from two Chinese immigrants in Korea. He told me that one man was a tailor, by trade, who taught him the forms of the system. The other teacher taught him weapons.

At a demonstration at a tournament, he came out dressed in his Kung Fu uniform (he told me that neither Byung Jik Ro or Ki Whang Kim knew that he was also studying Kung Fu) and performed for them. He told me that he was very nervous, because neither of them knew about his Kung Fu training, but that after he finished performing, they gave him their blessings and were impressed by his skills.

Grandmaster Young Pyo Choi performs Kung Fu for the first time in front of his seniors at a tournament in 1974.

When Grandmaster Young Choi came to Indianapolis, he had his heart set on building his own branch of the OMAC

Chapter 19. ABOUT MY TEACHERS

(Oriental Martial Arts College). He basically wore his Kung Fu uniform all the time, even while teaching Tae Kwon Do. I have old 8mm film footage from my first test from white belt to yellow belt in 1983, and in this video Grandmaster Choi performs a double broad sword form, a long staff form and So Ho Yun. At that time I had no idea how fortunate I was to capture these on film!

Unfortunately, if you are old enough to remember those 8mm movie cameras, the film only allowed for 3 minutes of recording before it ran out, and they were very noisy (if you listen to the sound of the projector in the background, during the beginning of the movie, "Enter the Dragon" where Bruce Lee and the English guy are watching film of the evil Han and O'Harra, you can get an idea of what the actual 8mm cameras sounded like when filming.) I only had a single roll of film with me and I wanted to be able to capture most of my performances at that test in 1983, so I only captured a little bit of Grandmaster Choi's performances. He was dressed in that same peach-colored Kung Fu uniform that I mentioned in my story, while everyone else was wearing the standard white Karate uniforms. V-neck uniforms were not yet available back then, and if they were, we didn't wear them.

Grandmaster Choi taught Kung Fu at 12pm Monday through Friday and Tae Kwon Do in the evenings at 5:30pm and 7pm. I trained with him during the afternoons during summers, and whenever there were days off from school, and basically lived at the Dojang from the moment school let out, until he closed in the evenings.

At that time, we received a lot of additional personal attention from Grandmaster Choi because he still had a strong passion for teaching and his school was still in its infancy. I enrolled with him in March of 1983 and was his 56th student to enroll in his school. We were each given a unique student identification number that was like a martial arts social security number (something that I have continued to use in my own schools up to this day). My number was WT83056, which meant that I trained at his WEST side location (hence the "WT") and I joined in the year 1983 (hence the "83") and was student number 56 (hence the "056"). He opened a 2nd location on the north side that was much smaller than the original school, but spent the majority of his time at the West side school. When I became a red belt, I was placed in charge of opening and teaching at the north side location for him.

Eventually, Grandmaster Choi decided to cancel his afternoon Kung Fu class because it was not growing. People were much more interested in Karate at that time, due to the release of "The Karate Kid" in 1984, just 2 years after he opened in Indy.

So, all the parents began searching for a Karate school and their very own Mr. Miyagi. Fortunately, Grandmaster Choi's sign read, "Korean Karate," and he was Asian. The public didn't know the difference between what they saw on the movie screen and what they saw in most schools. At any rate, his school began to grow by leaps and bounds. One of my tasks, to help with my tuition, was to stuff and fold fliers and then place them under people's windshield wipers in any parking lot I could find and to ask stores to allow me to post them in their window or leave them on their counters.

When he cancelled his Kung Fu class, I was left to continue my Kung Fu training with a few fellow classmates who kept

Chapter 19. ABOUT MY TEACHERS

the art alive in Grandmaster Choi's school and through personal instruction from him from time to time.

As the school began to grow, Grandmaster Choi began to filter some of his Kung Fu material into his Tae Kwon Do curriculum so that his students would have a more robust background than just a single art; and he treasured the Chinese arts and thought that every student should have some training in them. To his credit, he just added it in and told the students that these things were part of their training.

He never told anyone what was what. He never told us when we were learning something from Kung Fu, Karate, Hapkido, Judo, etc... and, as a result, nobody questioned it or had any problems with it. On T.V. we also were treated to the weekly "Black Belt Specials" or "Kung Fu Theater," which was a weekly showing of a Chinese Kung Fu movie; the ones where the dialogue was dubbed into English and made for a lot of fun when goofing around with my martial arts buddies (you know, the ones where the movement of their lips didn't match what was being said). So, there was a lot of exposure to Chinese Kung Fu at that time, and Bruce Lee, even though already dead for 10 years, was still a very hot topic around most of America; and of course, Jackie Chan was still making Kung Fu movies back then, too.

We didn't have the internet, and there were very limited resources at the local library. Maybe only 2 or 3 books on martial arts; and they were mainly Judo and Karate basics. So, we just trusted what our master taught us.

We were taught the basic Kung Fu stances and we performed them at the beginning and end of every class. We also learned a 2-man set that we often practiced at summer camps and outdoor training. Master Choi would really get into teaching Kung Fu at these events since he was the most experienced of the masters in the Chinese arts. Even the other masters and grandmasters paid very close attention when he taught this material, and looked forward to the opportunity to learn.

He also made sure to include his pride and joy, So Ho Yun, as a required form for his 2nd degree black belts, along with Pal Dan Kum Bong (a Sip Pal Gi long staff form).

Around 1988, the time that Tae Kwon Do had been included in the Pan Am games, he and his brother changed their signs from Korean Karate to Tae Kwon Do to capitalize on the new-found familiarity with all the coverage in the media.

Shortly thereafter, he began making small changes to the curriculum. He took out all of the Tang Soo Do 3-steps (which were self-defense techniques that were performed by having your opponent step forward 3 times while you stepped back 3 times and blocked each of the oncoming punches. On the 3rd punch, you blocked and then did your actual self-defense countering techniques on your opponent—a standard practice in many Tang Soo Do schools even to this day), and he replaced them with simpler one-step sparring techniques that are more in line with what many TKD students perform today.

He replaced some of the more obscure blocks with more standard Tae Kwon Do blocks, but he also began including Hapkido techniques at the intermediate level, and he also snuck in several Kung Fu self-defense maneuvers to our self-defense requirements. Again, nobody really knew the difference and we simply thought we were learning pure Korean Karate or Tae Kwon Do.

Chapter 19. ABOUT MY TEACHERS

Grandmaster Choi occasionally got a request from a prospective student about Kung Fu-only classes, but he always managed to talk them into joining his Tae Kwon Do program, until 1998. A Middle-Eastern man about my age came in to inquire about Kung Fu. In the yellow pages ad---(remember those?) he advertised that he taught Tae Kwon Do, Karate, *Kung Fu,* Tai Chi, and Hapkido. The average person didn't realize that he meant that these were integrated into one art (Moo Jung Ryu), and they would often come in looking for one specific art, thinking that they were taught at separate times.

At any rate, this gentleman and his wife were adamant about learning Kung Fu. They simply wouldn't be swayed, and I guess their excitement about wanting to learn Kung Fu re-ignited Grandmaster Choi's own excitement for it and he agreed to begin teaching it again. He began classes on Mondays and Wednesdays at 8:30pm.

At that time, I had already had my own school operating for 3 years, so I was not able to be at his school as often. Luckily, I was there when he agreed to begin the classes, and he let me know that he'd like for me to be there if possible.

I was thrilled, and began attending the classes again each week. He then started teaching Kung Fu classes at his North side location on Tuesdays and Thursdays at the same time. So I made sure to begin attending those as well, turning over my later classes at my own school to one of my senior-ranking students and then darting up to his school in time for the Kung Fu classes.

At that time, I was still competing and I soaked up all the training I could.

This time around though, Grandmaster Choi began staying dressed in his Tae Kwon Do uniform and taught the Kung Fu classes that way, while all the students were dressed in *Kung Fu* uniforms and wore sashes instead of belts.

He and his brother each host annual tournaments and Grandmaster Choi always wore either his silk peach-colored Kung Fu uniform (with no sash) or a white silk Kung Fu uniform for all of his performances.

Around the year 1997 or 1998 he took his white silk uniform and had one of my students alter it so that it was a standard Karate uniform for the top, but kept the pants the way that they were, but modified the ankle area slightly; then he wore his Tae Kwon Do belt with the uniform. He took his peach-colored Kung Fu uniform and had it altered as well by having a little green v-shaped cape-like piece added to it, so that it resembled more of what you would see on a "ninja" uniform around the back of the neck area.

I believe he had his uniforms modified to represent the blending of the arts in his system of Moo Jung Ryu.

He wore these uniforms on special occasions, like black belt tests, tournaments, demonstrations, etc....

As you now know, I left his organization in 2003 so I'm not certain about whether or not he is still teaching Kung Fu at either of his schools.

I was also fortunate enough to receive training with his brother, Grandmaster Joon Pyo Choi, in Columbus, Ohio. Grandmaster Joon Choi hosted an annual summer camp that I began attending in the early 90's each year until 2003. He also hosted a Spring training camp, a Fall training camp, and a Winter training camp.

Chapter 19. ABOUT MY TEACHERS

James Theros with Grandmaster Joon Pyo Choi, 1997

At these camps I was taught by Grandmaster Joon Choi, in a variety of subjects, including Kimoodo, his own Qi Gong (Chi Gong) system. It was also at these camps that Grandmaster Young Choi would open up quite a bit and teach me things from the Kung Fu system that he rarely shared outside of these camps and rarely with anyone below the rank of 5th degree black belt, including his broadsword and straight sword forms.

Grandmaster Joon Pyo Choi was invited by the Korean government to come to America and teach Korean martial arts. He came over in 1971 and began looking for a place to open his school. He tried a couple of different locations until he finally ended up in Columbus, Ohio and opened the first American branch of The Oriental Martial Arts College.

Grandmaster Joon Pyo Choi also trained in Kung Fu, although I don't know to what extent. Around the time that the shift from Korean Karate/Tang Soo Do was being made in the organization, Grandmaster Joon Pyo Choi began creating some of his own curriculum (from his own personal system, known as Moo Gong Ryu--- "Guardian of The Peace System") and replaced much of the former curriculum with his own personally-created material.

Grandmaster Joon Choi's material has a strong Chinese influence in it and he has created some of the most beautiful forms I have ever seen. His personally-created forms always scored well in competitions, particularly open-style competitions, and he went on to become a great coach for Tae Kwon Do athletes. He was the coach at the 1988 Pan Am games and coached Herb Perez (the first TKD Olympic Gold Medalist ever), and produced great champions like Greg and Doug Baker, Chris Spence, and Greg Fears (another student of Sip Pal Gi under Grandmaster Young Choi).

In 1983 Chris Spence came to live with Grandmaster Young Choi for a while and helped him teach classes. I remember being in awe as Chris held his side kick "straight" up to the ceiling and held it there for minutes at a time, without even stretching! I wanted to be able to do that and worked as hard as I could to make it a reality.

Unfortunately, in the process, during a partner stretch, I tore cartilage in my right hip and it has hindered my flexibility ever since. I was able to get into a full split (sorry, no picture

Chapter 19. ABOUT MY TEACHERS

to prove it) but, rather than easing out of the stretch I quickly jumped up and felt the tear, in the joint; I developed a loud *popping* sound in the hip, as a result.

When Grandmaster Joon Choi invited Grandmaster Young Choi to come to America, they began creating spectacular demonstrations. Both of them wore their Kung Fu uniforms at these demonstrations and performed many 2-man fighting sets, including an exciting long-staff fight that I was privileged to learn 3 sections of and still teach to my students from time to time. Grandmaster Choi was gracious enough to allow me to capture this on film at a summer camp one year, for future reference.

According to Grandmaster Young Choi, he and his brother were performing at Madison Square Garden, in New York in the late 1970's, and a film company was producing a documentary. They filmed several demonstrations of the Choi brothers, but when it was completed, the film crew labeled their art as "Karate," which insulted them so they supposedly pulled out of the project.

That was unfortunate, because who knows what may have happened with their careers if they had been included in that project?

Grandmaster Joon Choi was in an unfortunate car accident and injured his back in the mid 80's, which prevented him from performing at demonstrations, so he stepped aside and allowed his brother to take center stage for all of the demonstrations, while he went to work on creating his "Kimoodo" system, with the purpose of rehabilitating his body.

Grandmaster Joon Pyo Choi is widely known for teaching a form known as Sorim Jang Kwon (Shaolin Chang Quan, in

Brothers Grandmaster Joon Choi and
Grandmaster Young Choi, Circa 1988

Chinese), which translates to Shaolin Long Fist. This particular form, which is very popular in many Kang Duk Won systems, and many Tang Soo Do systems, draws its roots from the same place as Korean Kung Fu (Sip Pal Gi).

Sorim Jang Kwon is a two-man form, in which it appears that the partners are engaged in mortal combat. It is a very beautiful form to watch and is very similar to the form Chung Nyun Kwon (Ching Nian Quan), which means "Youthful Fist." I have video footage of Grandmaster Joon Choi demonstrating this form with his student, Greg Baker at his annual Battle of Columbus martial arts tournament in 1984.

As a side note, one of my other instructors, Grandmaster

Chapter 19. ABOUT MY TEACHERS

Kang Rhee, also teaches this form in his Pasa Ryu system, in Memphis, Tennesee.

Grandmaster Joon Choi and his brothers originally lived in North Korea and fled to South Korea during the Korean War, where they spent time in a refugee camp, before settling down in Seoul, Korea, and then coming to America in 1971.

In 1990, while working at Grandmaster Young Pyo Choi's school, I saw an envelope in the trash that had a picture of someone I recognized from reading many issues of Black Belt Magazine and Tae Kwon Do Times.

The envelope contained an invitation to a Bill "Superfoot" Wallace seminar to be held on the north side of Indianapolis. I took the invitation and went, with the sole purpose of meeting one of my childhood idols.

I had seen Bill Wallace in the movie, "A Force of one" with Chuck Norris, and also in the movie, "The Protector" with Jackie Chan.

I had also closely followed his fighting career and had pictures of him, kicking sky high, posted on my bedroom walls, alongside pictures of Bruce Lee. He was one of my main inspirations when it came to kicking and flexibility and I wanted to be able to perform kicks the way that he did.

When I went to the seminar I was introduced to a completely new world. Prior to that event, I had very limited experience and knowledge of anything martial arts related that didn't occur with the walls of Grandmaster Choi's school. It was an eye-opening experience, and led to a long-standing relationship with Bill that has lasted to this day.

I kept in touch with him and I did a brief teaching stint with a group called the Young Americans, which was a group

James Theros & Bill "Superfoot" Wallace, 1990

of martial arts instructors who taught Karate classes at local YMCA's, YWCA's and local Parks and Rec places. Bill was also good friends with the Indiana director of this group, Rick Tague.

Bill Wallace was originally from Lafayette, Indiana and studied under Grandmaster Glen Keeney. So, he regularly came to visit Karate schools here in Indianapolis and I went to each event that he was present at. I used to travel to a friend's school each Wednesday, Hanshi Herb Johnson, and spar with their Karate fighters to that I could get some cross training.

One evening I had the privilege of traveling to Lafayette, Indiana to partake in a special seminar that Bill was teaching just for the instructors involved in the Young Americans program. During the seminar, we got to gear up and actually spar each other, while Bill gave us instructions on how to improve our sparring.

Chapter 19. ABOUT MY TEACHERS

We lined up in two long lines and rotated after each match. Then, lo and behold, Bill Wallace joined the lineup as well, with sparring gear on, which meant we each got a chance to spar the champion! It basically ended with me getting schooled in the art of kickboxing by the legend. I was scared to really try anything because I was worried he might try and knock me out to teach me a lesson!

After that evening, we went out for dinner and drinks. I traveled with Bill for two years and worked as his assistant at the seminars he taught and received personal instruction from him along the way. I had him out to my school to teach seminars as well. He is usually known for teaching flexibility and kicking, but he also taught a wonderful boxing and wrestling seminar for us.

In 1997, as I was in the prime of my competitive days, I learned of a competition in Phoenix, Arizona that was being hosted by a Chinese master named Li Jin Heng. I was excited to go and compete at his event since it was a Chinese Kung Fu tournament, but I mainly wanted to go because of a seminar that was listed on the registration form. The seminar was being conducted by Master Kenny Perez.

I had ordered several VHS tapes of Master Perez, mainly weapons videos, to learn some additional information about the weapons that I was learning from Grandmaster Choi. I have always been a serious student and I have always done extensive research to learn more about the subjects that I am learning.

So, I flew out to the competition and competed. I was very excited to meet Master Perez and it turned out that I was the only person who registered for his seminar. Rather than cancelling it, Master Perez gave me a private 2-hour seminar that day.

Korean Kung Fu: The Chinese Connection

James Theros, Choi Young Pyo, Bill Wallace, 2000

Bill Wallace and the Author, 1998

Chapter 19. ABOUT MY TEACHERS

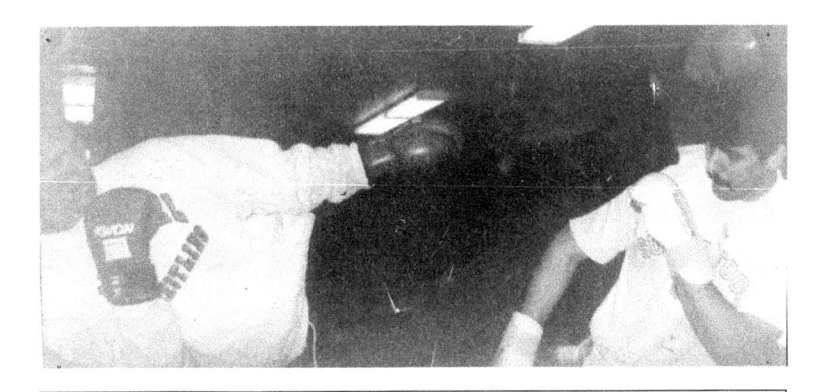

Bill Wallace and the Author in a sparring session, circa 1995

James Theros with the Parents of Bill Wallace, circa 1995

I got his contact information and the next month I flew back out to begin training with him. He was very hospitable and allowed me to stay at his home with his family for a few days. We trained at a local park during the day and I attended his classes at his school during the evenings.

Master Perez began teaching me Wushu, along with the traditional forms of his system.

Master Perez trained with Sifu Douglas Wong in the traditional Shaolin 5 Animals system, as well as with the Great Coach Wu Bin, in Beijing China.

Master Perez moved to China and lived there for two years during the mid-1980's and, while there, he met Donnie Yen and Jet Li while training with their teacher, Coach Wu Bin. Master Perez had a brief movie career in China and starred

Master Kenny Perez and James Theros Working with the Whip Chain, 1998

Chapter 19. ABOUT MY TEACHERS

alongside Donnie Yen in a movie called, "Mismatched Couples" and played in a movie called, "Dragon Fight" with Jet Li as well. He also did stunt work in the movie, "Revenge of the Ninja III" and did stunt work in Germany for a television series called, "Der Puma," in which he was the body double for the main star of the series.

Master Perez has been featured on the covers of many Kung Fu magazines and has written a monthly column for *Inside Kung Fu Magazine* for as long as I can remember.

At the time of this writing, I have been to China twice with Master Perez to train with his master and to experience Kung Fu in China. I use Master Perez as my go-to-guy for many things *Chinese*, and have been able to take advantage of our relationship to help uncover some of the answers about my

Donnie Yen, Kenny Perez, Jet Li, Coach Wu Bin, Circa 1985

Kung Fu system that my Korean masters were not able to answer.

Master Perez comes out to my school to host a seminar once each year and I travel to his home in Phoenix a couple of times per year to train with him there as well.

In 2003, upon leaving Grandmaster Young Pyo Choi's OMAC organization, I trained for a few years with Grandmaster Kang Rhee, who, consequently was one of Bill Wallace's

Assorted Photos from Training in China

Chapter 19. ABOUT MY TEACHERS

Assorted Photos from Training in China

Assorted Photos from Training in China

first teachers (and also taught Elvis Presley). Grandmaster Kang Rhee is based in Memphis, Tennessee and has created his own system, called, "Pasa Ryu" (The Way of Honor).

It is a blend of Karate/Tang Soo Do, Kung Fu and Hapkido. He still teaches many of the old-style two-man forms from Kung Fu, that are often taught in many Kang Duk Won systems (a very old Korean martial art). I chose to study with him because he taught a lot of similar things that I had learned from Grandmaster Young Pyo Choi. I eventually went on to earn my 4th and 5th Degree black belts from Grandmaster Kang Rhee.

Chapter 19. ABOUT MY TEACHERS

When I left the OMAC organization, I was only 30 days away from testing to my 4th Degree black belt. I flew down to meet Grandmaster Kang Rhee in person and discuss the possibility of joining his organization. After a lengthy conversation about why I left the OMAC organization, he accepted me as a student and began personally teaching me some of his material, including Sorim Jang Kwon, and allowed me to record all of his forms on video.

James Theros & Grandmaster Kang Rhee, 2003

The Author With Students of Kang Rhee

He is an amazing man. At 65 (back in 2003) he not only taught classes, but demonstrated forms and self-defenses for his classes each time I was there. He amazed me with his ability to walk out and sit down into a full split without warming up.

I became one of his students and learned a great deal of information from him. I still keep in contact with him and I send folks to his organization, the World Black Belt Bureau, because I have never met a man with better character and a genuine willingness to help others than him. He describes himself as an Christian first, an American second, and a Korean 3rd.

My next stop was, as mentioned in chapter one, to meet and begin my training with Grandmaster Na and Grandmaster Choi Byung Yil.

Grandmaster Byong Yil Choi Teaches James Theros at His School in California

Chapter 19. ABOUT MY TEACHERS

Since I have already covered them in chapter one, I will simply move ahead.

As I began traveling to California doing my Kung Fu training with Grandmaster Byong Yil Choi (pronounced Choy, and no relation to Grandmaster Young Choi) and Grandmaster Na, I drove out to Santa Monica to visit the beach and noticed Grandmaster Bong Soo Han's Hapkido school. He was another person that I had followed since my childhood.

Obviously, my first introduction to him came by watching the movie, "Billy Jack." I first saw it as a young child on HBO. From there, I saw him in the movie, "Force Five" with Joe Lewis, and in his comedic role in, "Kentucky Fried Movie." I also saw him on the covers of many martial arts magazines and purchased his book on Hapkido.

A Private Lesson with Grandmaster Bong Soo Han

Grandmaster Bong Soo Han and James Theros, 2005

At that time, I was training at a Hapkido school in Chicago, Illinois with Grandmaster K.S. Hyun. When I saw Grandmaster Han's school, I stopped in to meet him and possibly get a picture and an autograph. It occurred to me that it would be more economical for me to transfer my Hapkido training to his school, since I was already flying out every month for my Kung Fu training, and, I enrolled at Grandmaster Han's school and became one of his affiliate schools. I was one of Grandmaster Han's last students, because he passed away in January, 2007. I was only a month away from testing to 1st Dan in his system when he passed away.

Chapter 19. ABOUT MY TEACHERS

This, of course, left a gap that needed to be filled in my Hapkido training. Around 2002 or so, I had purchased a DVD series called, "This is Hapkido" featuring Grandmaster Yong Sung Lee.

I immediately thought of him and called to speak to him about my situation. He graciously spent 2 hours on the phone with me that day and I booked a flight out to Washington DC to go and meet with him in person.

After spending time with him in the office he had me demonstrate some of my Hapkido skills for him so he could get an accurate assessment of my skills. He then began to teach me some of the techniques from his system and I stayed and attended his evening classes.

He invited me to stay at his home and we spent many hours talking together about his World Mudo Federation. He accepted me as a personal student and as an affiliate. I began flying out to his school each month for training, and have continued to do so since 2007.

I was tested and promoted within his system and awarded the position of Secretary General for the World Mudo Federation. Then, in 2011 I was promoted to Vice President of the World Mudo Federation.

Grandmaster Yong Sung Lee created his own martial art system that he calls Hapmudo, which is a Hapkido-based art that includes elements of Kung Fu, Tae Kwon Do, Jiu Jitsu, Kickboxing and other arts as well as multiple weapons.

My background in Kung Fu was a perfect fit for his organization and I teach regular seminars on the Chinese arts for his students and other World Mudo Federation members and affiliates.

James Theros with Grandmaster Yong Sung Lee, 2007

I have been very fortunate to train with so many wonderful instructors, each of them adding something to my knowledge.

Chapter Twenty

An Interview with Grandmaster Na Hi Seup

I proudly present this interview from my Kung Fu Grandmaster. Actually, this interview was conducted in several parts, on several different occasions, over several years. I have pieced it together to try and create one coherent, compelling interview for the reader.

I had to translate a few of Grandmaster Na's thoughts into sentences and phrases that the average American can easily understand, while I have left other parts unchanged, because, while much of it is broken-English, it makes the point quite clearly. If you've spent much time speaking with Korean masters, you begin to understand some of their thoughts, almost as if it were another hybrid language.

Pay close attention to what you are about to read, because this is the first time in American history that such an interview has been conducted, and from such a person who was so close to the source and beginnings of this art in Korea.

"Praying Mantis was created by the first master, Wang Lang. Since then, the 2nd descendent and so forth, up to the 8th descendent, was Lim Poom Jang. He was born in Manchuria.

The 9th descendent, So Sin Dang (pronounced So SHIN Dang). While Grandmaster Lim Poom Jang opened his Kung Fu studio in Korea, in Seoul. Under his teaching, there were many famous Chinese martial arts men.

One of them is Lee Duk Kang. Before he changed his name to Lee Duk Kang, his original name was Yi Po Hyung; So, older people remember his name as Yi Po Hyung, not Lee Duk Kang.

Several famous guys were Doo Hak Jae, So Sin Dang, Yup Poon San.

So Sin Dang and Yup Poon San taught Praying Mantis and Shaolin; and they especially taught Shaolin Long Fist. That's why a lot of people remember Chang Quan Moon Pa. That means Chang Kwon Moon (Long Fist style). While he was teaching Chinese martial arts in Seoul, one of the famous Bagua teachers, No Soo Jun, and famous Praying Mantis guy, Kang Gyung Bang. The owner of the studio was Lim Poom Jang; his friend, Bagua master, No Soo Jun, and another famous Praying Mantis master, Kang Gyung Bang.

Under them; Lee Duk Kang, Doo Hak Jae, So Sin Dang, Yup Poon San. Especially this guy, So Sin Dan, learned all of these guys' arts; Praying Mantis from Kang Gyung Bang and Lim Poom Jang, and Bagua from No Soo Jun, and also, from Lim Poom Jang, Chang Kwon/Sorim Kwon (Shaolin Quan).

And, these two guys, Lim Poom Jang and Kang Kyung Bang, learned many weapons. There are another 3 famous students but, now, they don't teach students anymore

Chapter 20. An Interview with Grandmaster Na Hi Seup

because they made a lot of money in business.

Two of the guys died, and one of the guys opened an acupuncture practice. So Sin Dang is the only one left.

When they were taught Shaolin and Praying Mantis, by So Sin Dang, Yup Poon San, and Doo Hak Jae, the 10th descendant's name was Choi Byung Yil, who learned from them.

In this generation, many famous and strong guys, Choi Byung Yil, Yoon Ha Do, and I cannot remember the other guy. Many guys, now, next generation. The next generation will be the last group to study traditional Kung Fu, because, nowadays, Wushu has spread out all over the world; Wushu, plus original Kung Fu.

In the 1940's, and 1950's, there was a Chinese domestic revolution and Korean War. Especially in 1950, there was a Korean War. At this period, many famous Chinese martial artists immigrated to South Korea from the Shandong Peninsula, and, from 1957, they started to teach Kung Fu; but from 1950 to 1960, they taught only Chinese members. They didn't teach Koreans. In 1963 they started to teach Korean members, because, they needed money.

Even though we learned Kung Fu from them since 1963, they didn't teach high-level technique. They taught only Tan Tui; easy ones. Then, past 1970 they began to teach high-level technique. It took a long time for us to learn high-level Kung Fu from them (the Chinese).

For example, Golden Snake versus Crane, and Cho Gyo, I cannot remember Chinese pronunciation; maybe Jia Jio? Things like that.

Now we understood everything because it spread out since 1970 and it spread out all over Korea, but, even though they started to teach Cho Gyo, still, lots of people don't remember it and they didn't have a chance to learn it; because certain places, remote areas, they taught Golden Snake Versus Crane and Jia Jio. I believe that not many people understand that nowadays.

Lim Poom Jang showed many legendary things when he showed Tan Tui. When he hit the bo staff he cut it in half, he turned and it broke. He was very strong. He was the owner (of the school) and they were friends (referring to the other masters mentioned earlier).

I read an article in the newspaper about Moon Yong, in L.A. He wrote an article about his history and he learned from Kang Kum Bang, not Kang Kyung Bang. I guess he heard his name from somebody and he misunderstood; because if he learned from Kang Kyung Bang, he should have been taught Praying Mantis, but he doesn't teach Praying Mantis; and Praying Mantis has a policy of how to move, but, when I saw his instructors, even not one motion follow the policy. That means he created his forms. He didn't learn from Kang Kum Bang.

These guys (points to names of Lim Poom Jang, Kang Kyung Bang, No Soo Jun) they were friends. They were not exactly the same age, but, like 3 or 4 years difference.

Under them; Yup Poon San, So Sin Dang, Doo Hak Jae, Lee Duk Kang; they were students. The next students, Choi Byung Yil, Yoon Ha Do, like this (scribbles out rough lineage chart).

In those days, a lot of the schools had concrete floors. That's why many people ruined their knees. Including me (laughs). The best surface to learn Kung Fu is soil and clay because it absorbs the impact and nothing gets ruined.

Chapter 20. An Interview with Grandmaster Na Hi Seup

Lee Duk Kang's studio is like that; not concrete; not wooden floor.

Under So Sin Dang, he had famous Praying Mantis masters in Korea. Lim Poom Jang had a lot of students; but the story of quality is not good. If they learn for a long time they didn't say much, but, if they learned only 2 or 3 years, they say, "This is Kung Fu. This is Kung Fu." But, for a long time, then they shut up. (Author's translation: Grandmaster Na means to say that people who train for a long time don't feel the need to say too much, but those with limited experience feel the need to talk a lot). But, under his many students, they liked to show off. So, quantity? OK. Quality? No.

Even though he was one of the legendary, greatest Shaolin and Praying Mantis masters; just like, everybody knows him; everybody who learned Chinese martial arts, for even one day, everybody knows about Lim Poom Jang.

These guys, these guys only practice his age (points to Choi Byung Yil's name), my age now, who know them; but, Choi Byung Yil was actually in between this generation and this generation (referring to the generations of Lee Duk Kang and So Sin Dang; but he (points to Lee Duk Kang's name) was not the owner of the studio; Studio owner this (points to Lim Poom Jang's name), and then under him.

So, if they say, yes or no, we have to say, yes, they are his students; because he didn't run the studio by himself. They ran it together.

(Pointing to a map) This is South Korea. Japan is here. Taiwan is here. This peninsula is close to Korea (points to Shandong Peninsula). This peninsula we call Shandong. Shandong Peninsula.

Then there were the Arian tribes; some of them went

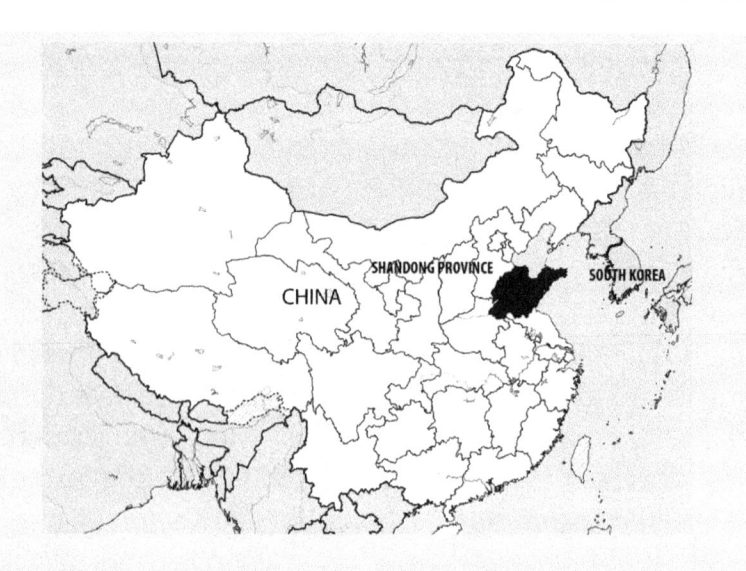

north. They are the ancestors of German or some European people. Some went to the south. They were the ancestors of the Tartaric, have you heard of the Tartaric people? Iranian, Armenian, Afghanistan.

This is China, right? Some of them went north to be ancestors of Europeans. Down here, this part (points to map) we call Hui Hui, the English name is Tartaric.

Ironically, the Tan Tui were created by these people (referring to the Tartaric or Moslem people).

Many people misunderstand Tan Tui. They think since it's a Chinese martial art that Chinese people made it, but Tan Tui was first time created by them. Hui Hui.

In Chinese letter, when we say, "onion," Hui People, because onions came from these people. When they created Tan Tui, you can see the original Tan Tui. Who's doing Yoga. His form is original. (Author's translation. Grandmaster Na means to say that the Indians who teach Yoga are the ones who still perform the Tan Tui's in their original form).

Chapter 20. An Interview with Grandmaster Na Hi Seup

Completely. From India, Bodidahrma came to China to spread and teach Buddhism.

The original Buddhism; Chinese Buddhism is one thing, same one, they believe the Buddha. But, the way to believe Buddhism is different. Big difference. India Buddhism and Chinese Buddhism are different. Korean Buddhism; little bit developed. We transferred Buddhism to Japan.

From a long time ago, Shandong Peninsula was famous for Praying Mantis. Praying Mantis and Gong Li, and (I don't know in Chinese letters), Sun Bin Kwon. Many famous martial artists lived here. Then, from this place (points to an area known as Changzhou, on the Chinese map) came Baji.

In the middle of China there is a river, a big river. Yangtze river. The martial arts practiced by the area north of that river we call Northern Kung Fu. It doesn't matter what family; Praying Mantis, whatever. Upside of the Yangtze River we call the northern Kung Fu.

South of the Yangtze River we call southern Kung Fu. Southern Kung Fu, including Nan Kwon, Choy Li Fut, White Crane, etc...

While the Northern part Kung Fu, they accepted Tan Tui from them (points to the map towards the Middle East). They developed it, just like they accepted Indian Buddhism; same way. As you know, while they are cooking Chinese food, they mix; mix a lot of things and one good taste. So, they accepted Tan Tui, but they developed it further.

As you've seen, Yoga's Tan Tui is very straight. One. Two; just like Tae Kwon Do. Chinese people thought about it. Those kinds of forms cannot make power. It looks like powerful, but, by the time you hit the target there is no power, so they changed it. They used to turn the waist, and a one hundred-fifty pound attack against a one hundred pound block, then the arm would be broken.

But 200 pound attack and 10 pound block; sideways, let it go. Go around. Then, I'll be ok. He will lose his balance; small investment; big pay.

That's the martial arts; so they changed Tan Tui a little bit. Even Tan Tui 6, they changed it a little by making it circular. When they changed the motion, they took advantage of turning power; that's the Chinese martial arts. While they were learning, they modified Tan Tui.

Nowadays, when we practice, it's the modified Tan Tui.

When it was the Qing (pronounced "Ching") Dynasty, there was one martial arts guy called, Soon Won Bin. I don't know if he escaped or immigrated; it might be that he immigrated, because Okinawan Island is small. Why did he immigrate? It might be because he fought with the royal family and ran away to Okinawa.

When he arrived in Okinawa, Okinawa was ruled by the Samurai. To control the Okinawans, the Japanese didn't allow them to carry swords, or any other weapons, but the Okinawans wanted to fight them. Constantly, one martial art from China, they learned from him (Soon Won Bin). It was the start of Karate.

They transferred Karate to the mainland. When they learned martial arts from him, it was close to Chinese martial arts, but, when they transferred it to the mainland; when they imported it from Okinawa, they modified it to Japanese style.

When you hear their sound, you can realize; Chinese people (speaks a Chinese word to illustrate the softness of how the language is spoken). Japanese people, all the time say, especially man, not woman; man, "Hai!" (Speaks a few words of staccato-sounding Japanese to illustrate the strictness of how it is spoken). Strict. While they are transmitting the art from Okinawa, just like Japanese-style, like this, like Karate. Ah. Tan Tui. Strict, strict, *strict*; not only their words, but also their lifestyle.

A palace in China; the roof looks like this (draws picture on white board for me). Very circular. Japanese Emperor's Palace (draws another picture), "Straight." Korean temples? Half. 100%, zero, 50%. While we were importing from them (Chinese and Japanese), we developed things a little bit, to suit our lifestyle.

Then, when we transferred it to them, they accepted like this, "Straight." Just like their pronunciation. "Hai! Hai! Hai!"

Martial art is same thing. From 1910 to 1945; thirty five years, the Japanese ruled; controlled Korea.

In the meantime, many, many people were educated by Japan. Unfortunately, including martial arts guys; they didn't go to Japan to learn martial arts on purpose. They went to Japan and they saw what they were practicing and they didn't know what it was, but later, they knew it was Karate. They practiced there for a long time; 10 years or 20 years.

Some guys practiced Aikido. Some guys practiced Karate. Some guys Aikido, they practiced it. Then in 1945; freedom.

Because American bombs were dropped in 3 places in Japan. The Japanese king surrendered.

In 1945, people went back to Korea, but they know only one thing; martial arts. They taught it to Korean people. Karate. But, they changed the name to Tae Kwon Do. Aikido people, they changed the name to Hapkido.

The first time, when they taught (speaking of the first

Korean masters who began teaching martial arts after World War II), it was 100% exactly Karate forms. There were no Tae Kwon Do forms before that. Hapkido? Exactly the same. It was 100% Aikido.

Many Tae Kwon Do people, say, "No. Tae Kwon Do was from Taekkyun. It originated from Taekkyun."

But, have you seen TaeKkyun? Taekkyun is close to Kung Fu. Nowadays, they changed it, the Tae Kwon Do forms, a little bit. To make some forms, high-class black belts (3,4, or 5 of them) had a conference. They made new forms in a couple of hours (referring to the creation of the Palgwe, Tae Geuk, and ITF forms of Tae Kwon Do).

Do you believe that's the proper way to make a form? No.

Even a Tai Chi form is more than 2,000 years old. They developed it; fixed it; cut things; added things. Fixed; fixed; fixed; fixed.

Now, finally, they made a Tai Chi form. Most of Kung Fu forms are more than a thousand years old. They fix, fix, fix, fix, fix; then, no more fix.

Tae Kwon Do forms, they still have to fix; because it's not the same way the lord created the universe.

Even though I'm an atheist, if the lord created the universe, it is perfect. Only man, human beings, make it worse. Tae Kwon Do forms, someday, they have to fix.

There was a Chinese revolution. Just like the American Revolution.

The communist party attacked one place in China. The Democratic Party fought with them, but, they failed; defeated. The Democratic Party fled to Taiwan.

In the meantime, people who didn't go to Taiwan, Yangtze River, the martial arts people who lived South of the river, escaped to Taiwan.

The Northern side of the river, at Shandong Peninsula, over here, (points to map) those people escaped to Korea; especially to Inchon.

When they arrived in Korea, they didn't teach Kung Fu to Korean people. It was kind of a "family secret." They didn't teach us.

Later, they needed money. They started to teach us. Later, then, Korean people went to them directly, to Shandong Peninsula to learn Kung Fu properly; Praying Mantis, Tai Chi, Baji, Bagua; here (points to Shandong Peninsula on the map.)

While we were accepting, Chinese Kung Fu from them, during World War II, we were ruled by Japanese people. Many people went to Manchuria. At the same time they controlled China; a lot of Japanese soldiers. So, our ancestors went to Manchuria, and they fought. In the meantime, they learned Sip Pal Gi.

Since I started Chinese martial arts, I tried to find what was the original. When I started, even though I tried to find a lot of books and things, or asking somebody else, they didn't know.

One conclusion I can make is that Sip Pal Gi has a lot of techniques from each family, like Tai Chi, Bagua, Baji, Xing Yi, those kind of family techniques were included.

So, I strongly believe that it wasn't one guy; maybe several of them, who created Sip Pal Gi; because it is very difficult to make one family martial art by just one guy; because so many different family martial arts are included.

To finish, even though I've practiced over 20 years, I believe that I've only learned 20%. I didn't mean weapon. I mean empty hand; fist; form; techniques.

A long time ago, Chinese martial artists traveled and met together and learned from each other. In the movie, "Fist of Fury," Bruce Lee got revenge for the death of his Grandmaster. His Grandmaster was real. In the movie; the story was real.

He was famous for Mi Zhong Nae, name of the Kwon Bup; Mi Zhong Nae.

He fought with the Karate Grandmaster. He hit him one time, one hit, and the Karate guy died.

So the Japanese doctors killed him with poisonous needles. That's why he died. At the time, he established Chinese martial arts center (referring to the Chin Woo Association and its founder Huo Yuan Jia). He had just established it; and then he died. The members developed the association and invited a lot of people.

They learned from Tang Lang, Praying Mantis, Shaolin; whatever. They absorbed a lot of things. We call Chinese Martial Arts Federation (referring to the Chin Woo Association).

Among the Chinese martial artists who were traveling to learn, other people family techniques killed some of them. So they mixed some of these techniques with theirs.

Even though it may be a Praying Mantis style, Praying Mantis has Sip Pal Gi techniques in it. Sip Pal Gi has Praying Mantis techniques in it. They give and take; not only Praying Mantis and Tai Chi; but not Baji. Baji was taught in a remote area. It was very difficult to get there. So, Baji was kept original for a long time.

When we say Baji, really, it's one shot one kill.

One of the most powerful Chinese martial arts is Baji; to get power, real power, in order to understand martial arts, they had to learn Baji. While they kept their own forms and techniques, other families, give and take, give and take. So, even though this is our own form; our own technique; it was too late; their forms already included other family's techniques.

While the Japanese people were controlling Korea, many people; many independent soldiers, went to Manchuria. From the Yangtze River, martial arts came here. The Koreans went there; they met together and trained together. They developed their skill.

Some guy created a family, like Praying Mantis or Tai Chi, they created one family. They called it Sip Pal Gi. Not exactly the roots.

It might be from Manchurian people.

Most people believe that they practiced when they were in Manchuria. So, before that, it was already created; and, Korean people, when they came back from Manchuria, after freedom from Japan; they brought Sip Pal Gi. Then they taught it to others.

Soon Bin Kwon and Tang Nang Kwon were imported directly from Chinese people. They taught us. The form techniques might be 90% pure. Like pure blood; they kept it pure.

Like So Chu Kwon, Ag Ga Kwon, Mei Hwa Kwon; we had to pay attention to the name of the form.

Ag Ga. I got an email from someone asking "what does Ag Ga mean?"

He might ask a Korean guy what Ag Ga means, but if the Korean guy doesn't know Chinese letters; in Korea, Chinese letters, then he might say, "Oh, it means, Terrible Family."

Think about it; why would someone name a martial arts form, "Terrible Family?"

"Ag" is a Chinese family name (Yue in Chinese); one who created a martial art.

"Ga" means family; so the name, just like, if you create your own martial arts form, then you could say, "Theros Family."

The man who has a family name, "Ag," they created a Kwon Bup (fist method); that's why he named it, "Ag Ga."

"So Chu", that's not the family name. "So" means small. "Chu" means reducing or reduction. "Ag Ga" is a family name; a martial arts family name.

Mei Hwa Kwon; same. Keum Gang Kwon; same.

So, while they were traveling, all over China, they met a lot of people and some guy chose the good movements; strong movements; and finally, they created one form, like "Ag Ga," "Mei Hwa," "Kum Gang."

So, I believe the guy who thought it was "Terrible Family" was not well-educated.

To understand Chinese letters, you must be educated. The guy heard the name, "Ag" which sounds the same in Korean and he guessed at it. If he or she were educated, then he or she would understand that it must be this (points to the Chinese character for family name), but only educated people know how to read Chinese letters.

For example, two weeks ago, a lady came to my studio, and I didn't ask her anything. She said she had been practicing Karate for 40 years. She asked me if I could teach her self-defense. I thought, even though she was a woman, compared to a man, it might be better than maybe 10 years of training for a man. Ok, a minimum of 10 years; she might have finished learning basic things. So, I figured I would start her from the middle level and I told her, "OK, I'll teach you."

Chapter 20. AN INTERVIEW WITH GRANDMASTER NA HI SEUP

After she changed into her uniform, she was trying to kick. If a martial arts man practices a long time, we don't need to fight. Just one punch or kick and you can see how long we practiced. Even though she said 40 years, to me, it looked more like 40 days.

But, it was already too late; I told her I would teach her.

So, by the time we got to self-defense, she didn't know anything at all; I had to start from the very beginning. It takes a long time to explain.

There were two Kum Do guys. One guy challenged the other. This guy cut a flower or a branch with his sword and he sent it to the other guy. He sent it to the guy's home town. After seeing it, the guy didn't want to fight anymore. By the time he got the flower; the cut, the angle; he saw it and realized that it was very done by a highly skilled swordsman.

Just watching someone kick one time, we know how many years they have been practicing.

My students knew that she was a YMCA Karate instructor.

It was right, but, her kicking technique? It was not very good. It was very, very difficult to teach her. One by one, by one, I had to explain.

Karate and Tae Kwon Do teach the same forms, same kicks, but no self-defense. Their self-defense is from Aikido.

Karate families; they have their own several families; Song Moo Kwan, Kang Duk Won, Chang Moo Kwan, etc....7 to 8 different Karate families. Then Kim Un Yong, ex-president of the Kukkiwon, he united them; one family.

When I was young, they taught their own style. Song Moo Kwan; Song Moo Kwan style Karate.

Kang Duk Won; Kang Duk Won style Karate. Not Karate. Kang Duk Won style Tae Kwon Do (Karate); but, exactly the same Karate. Karate forms, Karate kicks.

Kim Un Yong said, "This is no good. We have to be united." He asked each family, "Can you give your portion a little bit?" "Can you give your portion a little bit?" And, the masters said, "Ok, Ok, Ok."

Finally, they made one federation, (speaks very powerfully and in staccato-fashion), "Tae Kwon Do!" "Let's spread it out all over the world!"

To spread it all over the world, it must be easy to learn. If it's very hard, who's going to want to learn?

When we tested to black belt, we had to break red bricks; very difficult. Now, no one breaks those kind of things. So, easy to learn. That's why nowadays, there's a Tae Kwon Do studio on every corner.

There was a man, Choi Yong Eui (known better as Mas Oyama).

Before Tae Kwon Do, everywhere in the world there were Karate studios. A lot of people misunderstand about this man and thought he was a Japanese guy; but he was Korean (referring to Mas Oyama).

He went to Japan. He traveled all over the world, and fought everybody. He never failed. He fought the king of the Kick Boxers, King of Wrestling, King of Judo; King of whatever. He never failed. He won all the time.

That's why American people think, "Oh, Karate is the best!"

Everybody wants to be a famous singer like Elvis Presley, but, like Elvis Presley, this guy (Oyama) was the same. There was only one of him. No one can break his record.

While they were teaching Karate in Korea, it was only forms, kicks and punches and breaking; no self-defense.

Chapter 20. An Interview with Grandmaster Na Hi Seup

Self-defense came only from Aikido people. Ok, let's see where Aikido came from. If you go to school, if you go to elementary school, or high school, they will teach English, Algebra, German, or whatever. We say, "School."

If you go to a University they'll teach only one thing, but if you go to regular school they teach everything.

Karate, Tae Kwon Do, they taught form, kick, breaking, sparring.

When we learned Kung Fu, just like school; we learned Kung Fu forms, throwing, Shuai Jiao, Chin'Na, San Shou, Breaking, self-defense, weapons, etc.... that's why it's very hard to finish Chinese martial arts.

Tae Kwon Do and Karate, with only 5 years of training, you can teach someone.

It takes at least 20 years in Kung Fu because of all of the different elements of the art. Even Tai Chi, to teach someone, you must have 10 years of practice. Anybody can imitate, but not perfect it.

This is the difference between Tae Kwon Do or Karate, and Kung Fu. This is why Kung Fu studios are very rare.

Tae Kwon Do is everywhere; because, it only takes some people 3- 5 years to finish. That's enough time for most people to learn.

Kung Fu? If you practice for 10 years, you know 10 percent of what there is to know. 20 years, 20 percent. 30 years, 30 percent. But, most people, after 20 years, they stop studying and they don't practice anymore; which means they have reduced qualifications.

One excuse they use is aging.

They say, "Oh, I'm old."

So what; they still have to practice.

Then they can teach.

They have to have qualification to teach. But most people say, "I'm old. I have to stop. I'm tired."

Their abilities are reduced. They start to forget.

When I went to Korea last year, I stopped by to visit a friend and he asked me, "Do you remember that form? Can you remember that one?" I said, "Why?" He said, "I cannot remember it."

It was because he didn't practice.

Two or three years without practicing? You'll forget.

In regards to the form Ag Ga Kwon, there was a brave and strong General who was named Ag Be (Yue Fei, in Chinese). There was another guy, another General; and there was a king.

He said to the other General, "I'm Ag Be".

"You are competitor general;" and he told the king he was going to destroy his dynasty.

The other general told the king something bad about General Ag Be. So, he killed him.

Most people know that.

Since then, if you go to China or where Chinese people live, there is a temple. The tall and long beard, we call "Kwan Un Jang (referring to Chinese General Kwan Guan Yu)."

Confucius and Ag Be, the brave General, to honor him; he was very famous for his spear technique and martial arts. So, to honor him, I don't know who created Ag Ga Kwon, but, according to the legend, because we didn't live 2000 years ago, so, after the form was created, they adopted the name in his honor.

There are two reasons: Ag Be's name, or, Ga means family. My family name is Na. So, it would be "Na Ga Kwon" if I was the founder of a martial arts form. Then, I would put the name, "Na Family Fist."

Some people, when they created forms, didn't name the form. Just like when a baby is born, the parents think, "What name will be good for him?"

"John? Johnny? Carl? Kenny? Etc….. "

"Ok, let's choose Kenny. Ok. Your name is Kenny."

Then Kenny became his name. Before that, he didn't have a name. Just like this, somebody created one form and they think that it is a good form but have to decide on which name to give to this form.

Hok Ho Kwon, Sorim Kwon, Tien Soo, whatever; Ag Ga Kwon.

"Oh, Ag Ga is our celebratory or memorable, famous soldier. Ok, we'll use his name, Ag. Ga means family, Chuan; O.K., Ag Ga Kwon."

Ag Ga Kwon is not Praying Mantis. When Praying Mantis founder, Wang Lang, traveled the country, before he completed his art, he created his style, but it was still missing a few things.

Footwork, strong/soft, straight, turn; so, he had to gather more for his art; he traveled a lot. So, while he was traveling, 18 different families; Shaolin, this and that; before that there were some more families.

So, with the Praying Mantis as a foundation, he added some more things, from 18 families, including his forms. So 17 others styles had different techniques and his system didn't have too many things. So he put little things in from these other arts.

Between 1945 to 1949, from Shandong Peninsula, a lot of famous martial artists escaped to Korea, but most of them were Praying Mantis people; because Shandong is mostly

Praying Mantis. If Shandong was famous for Tai Chi, and people escaped from there to Korea, they would have taught Tai Chi style first, mainly, but, most of the people from Shandong were Praying Mantis people.

While they were teaching us, nobody knew Ag Ga Kwon. It had already been there in China or someone created it in Korea. Nobody knows; because it was already there before I was born and, at that time, Korean people who were trying to learn Chinese martial arts were not well-educated.

The problem is I had been practicing it for a long time, but I didn't know exactly what the name was. One form had a Chinese name, but still, I cannot remember the whole thing. I know that's Woo Gong Ga; "Oh that's Wun Han Ga", but, not completely.

If Korean people created it I might remember, "Oh that's that (referring to a name given to any particular form)." But, with a Chinese name, it's different.

"So, still, I don't remember the whole thing" (referring to other masters in Korea).

I was educated more than them. Still, it was confusing. Their grade level was about elementary school. How could they know?

They didn't have a chance to learn the real history, which transferred into the next generation of practitioners.

Back then, for our generation only, when we go to the studio, they told us not to speak. If we spoke, the master hit us; only physical exercise; only physical.

Exercise. Exercise. Exercise.

But, by the time we have to know what happened, before; I studied Chinese martial arts, some people died, some people stopped.

Chapter 20. An Interview with Grandmaster Na Hi Seup

Then we realized, some older martial arts man, who retired, said, there is a famous Mantis guy named Yoo Un Cho who lived in Korea, but moved back to Taiwan. While he was in Korea, he was a famous guy, and he helped, his portion to make strong, build Kung Fu for Korean people.

He analyzed and adjusted the information. He determined, "this is Ag Ga Kwon; this is So Chu Kwon, this and that, etc., etc., etc...."

So, we believe that he helped a lot. But I don't know how much; and, not only Praying Mantis.

The Praying Mantis part in Northern Korea was from Lim Poom Jang, Southern Korea was from Kang Gyung Bang.

While I was living in Seoul I was impressed with Lim Poom Jang. When I was living in Pohang, just a little north of Pusan, so, Southern, I was impressed with Kang Kyung Bang; because his instructors learned from him, left him and started teaching (on their own).

Lim Poom Jang's instructors also learned from him, left him, and started teaching.

So, we had a chance to compare Northern and Southern, and that's why, Ag Ga Kwon is in the Shaolin category; even though it still uses some Mantis techniques.

Before, even during our age (referring to his training as a youth), there was no book; no DVD; no T.V.

Only newspaper; but the newspaper didn't say anything about martial arts. So, for a long time, they could keep their family styles secret.

Shaolin stayed pure Shaolin. Mantis stayed pure Mantis. Baji stayed pure Baji.

All of a sudden T.V. came out, books got published, and the airplane, which allowed people to go to China right away.

So, in a short time, everything got mixed all of a sudden. Before, in order to learn, they had to walk; and from here (Indianapolis) to Los Angeles, it would take what? One year or two years? Then, come back? It's impossible; but to fly, it's only 3 or 4 hours, then, "Oh, they teach that? O.K."

Back before all of those things (books, DVD's, T.V., etc....) Then, they could lie and say, "I created this," or, "This is my secret."

A long time ago, it worked. But nowadays, it won't work.

Even right now people create forms, so, it gets mixed with so many things.

Just like your student, Matt. He said he had too many things in his brain after training earlier today (referring to the amount of information that was taught to him in a single session).

But, before, it was a little bit simpler. And with Yoo Un Cho; who was supporting us, and he analyzed things and categorized them, saying, "This one is Shaolin, this, this, this, etc...." Just like one form has a name.

So, getting back to the story, he; not only him, while they were teaching the Koreans these forms they decided to create the names for the forms and started using them. That's all I know. I cannot confirm whether this is true, though; so, nobody really knows. I was not born at that time.

For Mei Hwa Kwon, there are 3 different Mei Hwa's.

Praying Mantis Mei Hwa and 7-Star Mei Hwa.

Praying Mantis Mei Hwa and 7-Star Mei Hwa are in the same category, but, Praying Mantis Mei Hwa and the Mei Hwa that was created by Kang Hwa Ryung is different.

Wang Lang was the founder, Kang Hwa Ryung was, I think, the 6th or 7th generation from Wang Lang. According

Chapter 20. AN INTERVIEW WITH GRANDMASTER NA HI SEUP

to history, he was shorter than me (Grandmaster Na is approximately 5'5" tall) and fat.

People laughed, and said, "How can those kinds of men practice Praying Mantis? It should be impossible," but, his movement was very fast, like thunder.

So, after he learned Praying Mantis, he created another Mei Hwa form; but, the form he created, he put in the Mantis category.

And, Shaolin has a different Mei Hwa Kwon that we are learning. So that's a different Mei Hwa Kwon from Praying Mantis.

Kum Gang Kwon is completely Praying Mantis. People misunderstand. The reason people misunderstand is, I believe, that while the Chinese masters were teaching the Korean guys, they taught very fast, and, because the Koreans were not well-educated, they could not learn quickly.

To teach slowly, it takes a long time. So, they reduced the speed a little bit (meaning they reduced the speed of the movements in the form). Not regular speed. That's why, nowadays, students perform the form at a slower speed and, many places teach Kum Gang Kwon, so people misunderstand and think, "Oh, Kum Gang is Shaolin." Shaolin has a Kum Gang Kwon (Jin Gang Quan in Chinese), but the form we are learning is from Mantis; straight from Lim Poom Jang.

The reason why some schools teach more Praying Mantis forms (or have more Praying Mantis influence in the curriculum) is because it's a school, like any school.

In the school, you have a principal. The principal makes the decision about the curriculum. The curriculum is set out and the students have to follow it. The students don't know the difference. That's it.

Instructors, at that time, this guy (points to Lee Duk Kang's name), he worked with Lim Poom Jang. Lim Poom Jang died by the time I finished my military service training, around 1981 or 1982. When I finished my service training, Lim Poom Jang died.

While Lim Poom Jang and Lee Duk Kang were running the Kung Fu school, Lim Poom Jang taught strictly Mantis. Lee Duk Kang taught Long Fist, the Shaolin part. So, that's why they affected it. Shaolin and Mantis were taught together; and the main root should be Mantis form; even though there was a Shaolin form, they might have changed it with Mantis, but nobody knows. I believe that.

Kerro Kwon is affected by Praying Mantis. Somebody said the Kerro Kwon is completely Praying Mantis but, I don't believe that. Maybe 70% Mantis and 30% Shaolin mixed together.

I had 3 teachers. One guy came straight from Lim Poom Jang, and one guy came from Kang Kyung Bang; his name was Yoo Jae Doo; and he taught us. I had to move to different areas for work; and, actually, Master Choi Byung Yil was not a master in the studio at that time. He was just an instructor.

Doo Hak Jae and Choi Byung Yil were the same level. So, I was not completely the next generation. I was in the middle; but, I couldn't say, Choi Byung Yil is almost my same level; I couldn't say it, because I was in the middle; between. So, to respect Choi Byung Yil, I had to step down a level.

The Southern part of South Korea, while I was in Pohang, or while I was in Seoul, my hometown is Inchon, there was a master who famous for Praying Mantis. A lot

Chapter 20. An Interview with Grandmaster Na Hi Seup

of Chinese people escaped to Incheon. So, actually, I had 4 different masters.

The 4 places I learned were, Seoul, Pohang, Incheon, and Yecheon.

Yecheon is famous for porcelain.

Actually, I met 4, but, I didn't train with the master I met in Yecheon for a very long time. I can say he was my master but, maybe for only about 1 and a half years, so, I don't really count him.

For the form So Ho Yun, there are 3 So Ho Yun forms.

In Praying Mantis there are So Ho Yun, Joong Ho Yun, and Dae Ho Yun; Small Tiger, Middle Tiger, Big Tiger; they have 3 Ho Yun.

So Ho Yun is kind of famous. Just like there are many types of cars, but, still, people know that Mercedes is good. Then, another car company decided to make their own version of Mercedes, but they called it BMW, or Lexus.

So Ho Yun; Ho means tiger, but, originally, it was Xiao Hua, what's the name of the bird, the one that flies north in autumn, we call them Kyrogi, in Korean. Chinese people like birds, and the name So Ho Yun came from them.

But, at some point, someone started using tiger instead of bird. I don't understand why, but, all of a sudden, people started using Tiger/Ho.

After learning So Ho Yun, I learned Golden Snake Vs. Crane. Then time passed and I learned Tien Soo. It's nice and strong. I don't know where it came from, but I'm sure that Tien Soo is in the Shaolin category.

Most martial arts are affected by Praying Mantis because Praying Mantis has many good things. So, everybody takes a little bit of it to add to their own art. That's the reason, I guess.

I learned Jee Chuan (Jie Quan in Chinese) when I lived in Seoul. It comes from the same lineage as Tien Soo. First I was in Seoul, then Incheon, Pohang, and then Yecheon. Then, Seoul again.

First, I learned Jee Chuan, and Attack and Defense 1-6 (a 2-man set), then Tien Soo and another form, just before I came to the United States.

Korea is not as big as China, so Northern and Southern areas don't really matter. They teach similar systems there, unlike in China, where you have the Northern styles and the Southern styles.

(End of interview)

Chapter Twenty-One

An Interview with Master Choi Bok Kyu

Master Choi Bok Kyu is a Korean master and is the Korean equivalent of me. He is a martial arts historian and researcher, as well as a practitioner himself. Master Choi is approximately my same age (I was born in 1969). He studied Korean Kung Fu as a youth, as well as other ancient Korean arts, and then, with the aid of other Korean masters, he began helping to preserve an indigenous ancient Korean martial art, known as Sippalgi. I will use the term, "Sippalgi" when referring to the art that he teaches, and the term, "Sip Pal Gi" when referring to my system of Korean Kung Fu during this interview.

The art of Sippalgi was preserved in a manual called the "Moo Ye Dobo Tongji," which translates to, "Comprehensive Illustrated Manual of Martial Arts."

During my research, many years ago, I stumbled upon this work and was curious about it, because, while there seemed to be a lot of similarities between Sippalgi and Sip Pal Gi, there was a distinctive difference in the uniforms, the weapons, and some of the additional skills that were not being taught in Sip Pal Gi.

I visited many Korean websites and researched this art, still unsure about whether or not it was the root of Sip Pal Gi, after all, it basically had the exact same name. I downloaded several documentaries on Master Choi Bok Kyu's Sippalgi, and I saw some things that were nearly identical to what we practiced in Sip Pal Gi; most notably, some of the 2-man sets. I saw a video of Choi Bok Kyu and another master performing 8-step, exactly as we performed it in our system. I also saw him demonstrating some of the same Tan Tui's that we practiced, and many of the movements resembled ours.

At one point, there was a DVD released called, "Sip Pal Gi: Korean Kung Fu." I immediately ordered a copy and began watching it. Everything I saw looked to me like Sip Pal Gi, and the DVD showed all of the same basic stances (albeit, they stood a bit higher in their stances than we do), and I saw nearly all of our Tan Tuis on the DVD, several 2-man sets, including 8-step and Pe So Kwon (8-step #2), although there were extra movements added to the end of Pe So Kwon that I was unfamiliar with.

There were also several others, and one that I remembered seeing in the documentary that I downloaded from a Korean website.

There was also a short Korean master who was dressed in a gray Korean Hanbok, which is the same style and color of uniform that Grandmaster Na Hi Seup wears.

I thought I had finally found the connection I was looking for, yet, I still wasn't sure, because of the inclusion of some of the ancient Korean sword techniques, and the uniform that Choi Bok Kyu was wearing looked more Korean than Chinese.

So, in 2011, I got into contact with Master Choi and booked a trip for my wife and I to fly out and visit with Master Choi and his wife for training and research. We spent approximately a week in the Netherlands, and Master Choi was gracious enough to conduct this interview with me, as well as to teach me some of the pieces of his art.

Chapter 21. AN INTERVIEW WITH MASTER CHOI BOK KYU

I think you will find this interview to be very interesting, and I believe it will help clear up some of the confusion that I had, and that other researchers may have when comparing the two arts of Sippalgi and Sip Pal Gi.

Here is the interview in its entirety. I have only made minor modifications to the wording, because Master Choi speaks English very well and he was very easy to understand.

Anyplace where I asked a specific question is listed as "Author."

Author: What can you tell me about Sip Pal Gi?

Choi Bok Kyu: Sip Pal Gi. The name itself is more related to Korean history. Those teachers don't use the name Sip Pal Gi. That's what we can find. Master Lee (referring to Lee Duk Kang), and then he called his art something else, but he doesn't call it Sip Pal Gi; and then, Master Lim (referring to Lim Poom Jang) calls his art "Tang Lang," and he doesn't use the name Sip Pal Gi.

And there are some others, Pal Gwe Jang (Bagua Zhang) in the Incheon area, and there's No Su Jun (famous Bagua master), and there's another one in Pusan and they are mostly Tang Nang Kwon (Praying Mantis), because Korea is very near Shandong.

Most Chinese people in Korea, they come from Shandong. Shandong is very near Incheon, so with the inner trouble in China, there was inner trouble in China with the Communist party, so then more people came from there at that time. They wanted to avoid all the trouble.

There were some Chinese people before that, but somewhere around the 1950's, a little bit earlier, or after. When they started teaching Kung Fu, many Koreans learned the art from them, and then they named it Sip Pal Gi.

Master Lim Poom Jang was very influential. I think he was a professional teacher; all the others had jobs. They ran restaurants or something like that, but Lim Poom Jang and Lee Duk Kang were professionals; so they had a lot of students.

AUTHOR: So, I looked at a DVD you had created and I saw something that you called, "Dan Kwon" on the DVD; but the Dan Kwon forms are the same as our Tan Tui's. So, how is it that your art of Sippalgi and my art of Sip Pal Gi, even though they are a bit different, they share the same basics?

Choi Bok Kyu: You can see that those are Tan Tui, here you have Tan Tui (points to a picture in a book on his desk). So, my grandmaster, when he started teaching, he used some of this material (referring to Kung Fu) for teaching.

Author: So, it didn't come from sippalgi? Did it come from Kung Fu?

Choi Bok Kyu: No. Sippalgi had no basics, and when he learned Sip Pal Gi it was a different system. So it wasn't like the current system; and, when he learned it, during the Korean War period, it wasn't in the same type of setting; like in a martial arts gym. So, at that time, he learned like that; and, he had a different system; so when he started teaching, he needed material.

In the beginning, he tried to teach exactly the same way that he learned and practiced, but the people didn't like it.

People wanted to learn more, just like nowadays. It's the same thing (referring to modern student's attitudes towards learning martial arts); but, what he learned, the way he practiced, it was very little, just a small amount of techniques and then all the variations and applications, etc...

Chapter 21. AN INTERVIEW WITH MASTER CHOI BOK KYU

But that way didn't work; and the people just wanted more and more.

Then, when he started teaching in 1970, the Chinese martial arts were just booming all over the world, you know, Bruce Lee and all that. So, whatever he tried to teach, people thought it was basically Kung Fu. So, he couldn't teach the way he wanted to teach.

He thought if the people want to learn these old techniques, so he taught them the old material (referring to Kung Fu).

He tried to teach his own material (referring to Sippalgi). I don't know if you know about this modern history, but, this martial art is very rare, only several, in Seoul; Master Lim Poom Jang, my Grandmaster, Kim Kwan Suk; and then there were only like 3 or 4, and all the Koreans wanted to learn more.

And there's a funny story about the time. There were some Chinese who had this martial art, but they were not professional instructors, so they ran a restaurant, a Chinese restaurant, and then the Koreans heard that they were martial artists, so they visited the restaurant and tried to ask if they would teach them Kung Fu, and they bought a lot of food (laughs).

So, in the beginning, the Koreans learned martial arts like that; but the Chinese didn't want to teach the Koreans; and I had the same, when I visited him (Lee Duk Kang) and he didn't want to show anything.

You can see that that is one of the basic Chinese attitudes. I can fully understand though, because Koreans are very much hostile, especially to the Chinese, and Koreans attempted to look down on them, although China is a very big country, but the Koreans had this attitude.

So, he explained that he practiced martial arts himself because this is a very tough country (referring to Korea, where Lee Duk Kang lives). So I can fully understand what he was saying. So he practiced for himself.

So, in a way, it's a little bit secretive. He practiced from like 2 pm to 4 pm, in the gym. He always locked the door. He practiced for himself, every day for at least 2 hours; except for teaching; and after that, he started teaching.

(Side note from the author: Lee Duk Kang is Chinese but lives in Korea).

So, anyways, the Chinese are like this, so, at that time, they thought to sell the art. So, one form, if you want to learn one form then you had to pay a lot.

So, in the early stage, when the Chinese art was transmitted to Korea, the Korean masters were kind of like Korean pioneers. They spent a lot of money, and, even though they spent a lot of money with them, the Chinese didn't teach them correctly. They purposely taught them differently from the Chinese students.

The student of Lim Poom Jang, So Sin Dang; I have his book, and in his book he said these things.

If you read the preface of his books, he said he used to teach in Korea and then he went back to Taiwan. And then he came back, and then he said he felt very sorry for the Koreans, because he didn't teach correctly. So he apologized and came back again to teach the real art properly.

So, that was their attitude in the beginning.

And these forms (pointing to a book we were looking at), some things were from those masters (referring to Lim Poom Jang and So Sin Dang), and then, they added some things

Chapter 21. AN INTERVIEW WITH MASTER CHOI BOK KYU

from books or other sources. So there was a lot of stuff mixed together. Then, they called it Sip Pal Gi; and it's like a Chinese Sip Pal Gi.

Author: So, did you have training in Korean Kung Fu?

Choi Bok Kyu: No, I'm a historian, so I collect all these books.

Author: I've seen some video of you performing things that look quite similar to the art that I study.

Choi Bok Kyu: So, in the martial arts, there are only so many ways to move the arms and legs, so there are some similarities, but, those basic combinations and techniques, as I explained; my Grandmaster took them and put them into our art.

And then, originally in Korea, Chinese martial arts, they didn't practice this way (referring to a video of himself performing a 2-man fighting set). So, my grandmaster added some things, and then, now it became Chinese; Chinese Sip Pal Gi, or all these things. Whenever he tried something and he lost everything (referring to his Grandmaster having to close his school, which you will read in a bit). So it became Chinese.

Mrs. Choi: That was also a melting pot during that time. Everything affected one another and nobody was really concerned about it.

Choi Bok Kyu: So, the style that you are practicing is Praying Mantis mixed with Long Fist.

Author: I saw somebody performing Ag Ga Kwon in a video from one of your public performances.

Choi Bok Kyu: These things were, at the time, we used them. Ag Ga Kwon, Ko Woo Kwon, So Chu Kwon, Kum Gang Kwon, Huk Ho Kwon, O Ho Kwon, all those things; we used to use those, and then, later, when the Grandmaster started teaching again, the situation changed.

So, now they started looking for the traditional martial arts, and, when he published his book in 1987 (Grandmaster Kim Kwang Suk), he closed his gym.

He tried, all through those years, but the students wanted to learn more techniques, and he explained that, from the 1970's, his art was from the Mu Ye Dobo Tongji, and he showed it, and people didn't want to learn so he closed his gym down in the early 1980's.

And then a scholar came and was looking for traditional dancing. He found out that traditional dancing was closely related to martial arts, so he found out that there was a master who knows the Sippalgi from the Muye Dobo Tong Ji, and he tried to show his appreciation towards Grandmaster Kim Kwang Suk and asked him to please open his school to the public. So, that's the reason he published his book in 1987.

After that, University students came to him. They wanted to learn and they wanted to organize a club in the University, and it changed his mind. From before that period, mainly people interested in fighting wanted to study martial arts, or in Korea in the 70's there were, not gangsters, but, some guys who wanted to show off, and there were many cases; but then it changed.

The University students and instructors were involved; so he published his book.

Author: So, before that time though, he used to teach the same material that I study?

Choi Bok Kyu: Yes, he used that material.

Author: Do you know who your Grandmaster's teacher in that art was?

Choi Bok Kyu: He didn't study as a formal student but he was friends with Lim Poom Jang. So, he used to visit there, at least, that's what I heard. Lee Duk Kang used to be the person who took care of the gym and so, Lee Duk Kang is older than Grandmaster Kim Kwan Suk, but Lee Duk Kang couldn't treat him like that, because he was a friend of his teacher.

There are many funny stories. One time he visited Master Lim's place, and Lee Duk Kang was outside the door, and then he said, "Come here, come here, I'm watching my master practicing." And then Grandmaster Kim said, "Hey, if you're not allowed then you better stop!" And he said, "Oh, it's fine (laughing)."

And, another story, Grandmaster Lim passed away, and his wife came to Master Lee Duk Kang's place to get some money back, because he bought the forms, but he didn't pay. So, Master Lim's wife came to get the money.

There were several gyms at that time, so when he (Grandmaster Kim Kwan Suk) started teaching, then many Chinese martial artists came and tried to learn, and they took it back with them, and they called it Sip Pal Gi. So, in the beginning, he taught those forms, the sparring forms (2-man sets), but it was hard to teach. You need two people to remember, and then they tried to learn it; so we still keep it, as our art.

Otherwise they call it Chinese.

So there are many things like that. So, at this moment, it's a little bit hard to tell which part is hard and rigid, it's really authentic Chinese, and which part is Korean contribution, and then what you call Korean Sip Pal Gi, you cannot find it in China.

China has already changed it to all the Wushu styles.

So, compared to those Wushu styles, or what they call, nowadays, the traditional art, I think this (referring to Sip Pal Gi) is better than what they are doing now. So, a lot of things are like that. But, you know, arts are always developing. They start it and then they build it up and they collected all those materials.

So, what Grandmaster Kim learned was not a "form" style. He was taught old style, technique by technique, but you can always connect those techniques as a routine form; but what he learned was a very small amount of techniques. That's old style.

Then, at that time there was No Soo Jun, and he had 6 or 8 forms of palm techniques, so, not so many. And then, there was another old master, Master Pan. He practiced in Japan. He was an old master of Aikijujitsu and he only had about 16 techniques. So, from these older master's perspectives, if somebody emphasizes 3,000 techniques, like in Hapkido, if they saw an advertisement, they would think that it was not a real martial art. The old masters believed that as long as you are good at something then you can do it perfectly; and then it was good; but today's people don't think this way.

Most people are looking for fun. So, we have to consider that aspect as well. And, Grandmaster Kim looks at the Dan Kwon (Tan Tui) as very useful. Very simple technique; punches and combination kicks, and some techniques you cannot avoid, because they are very common. So he organized them in our art.

So when we compare my style to your style, when we talk in person it's good. You can ask, and I have a chance to explain; so we can discuss and share each other's ideas and thoughts. But, otherwise, like on the internet, it's harder to talk and discuss.

Chapter 21. AN INTERVIEW WITH MASTER CHOI BOK KYU

So, we have our basic theory [in a particular system] and all of the movements are related to this theory. You need a theory to be able to explain your movements. After a while, if the theory is established, then it's easy to teach the movements. So, that's the difference between our systems.

Author: Are there forms in your system of sippalgi?

Choi Bok Kyu: Yes. We have forms from the Muye Dobo Tong Ji. That's what we do, and I organized some other forms for our students, some simple forms. So, for the beginners I use the Dan Kwon (Tan Tui) and I added some more, like 3 palms.

This book on [sippalgi] was created in the late 18th century. The earlier version was more technique by technique, more based on just fighting, and then gradually, it was formalized. And it was written almost at the end of this ancient style, because in the late 18th century they used firearms. So, that's the reason why there is so much emphasis on swordsmanship in Sippalgi.

Master Choi Bok Kyu and James Theros share knowledge together in Amsterdam, 2011.

All the other weapons became unnecessary. The sword is one of the only weapons you could carry. You could use the musket and still use your sword, so that's the reason it became more and more important.

And, then, just after the publication of this book (the Muye Dobo Tongji), they completely changed it.

At the end of the 19th century you didn't need all these martial arts for the military. It was the same in Japan. So, what we call the modern martial arts started at approximately that period.

And, then Judo came in the 20th century. So, they changed it. And then, the modern perspective was bare-handed techniques. So, you can look around at all the modern martial arts, like Tae Kwon Do, Karate, or Judo, Aikido; basically bare-handed techniques, because society changed.

Nowadays, people have this concept in their minds about the martial arts and when they see the ancient martial arts, then they use this prism; because ancient martial arts are different. They were more weapon-oriented. So there is some conflict; but the people usually don't recognize it.

They have this modern martial arts frame of mind, and then they look through this window to the ancient styles.

Author: So, why so much emphasis on weapons in your system still?

Choi Bok Kyu: Yeah, now, I emphasize the classical martial arts. One reason is for preservation but, modern martial arts already have had a 100-year history and people want to learn the original style. So, it's always like this. Bear-handed techniques are popular, and, I hope, the next step is that they are interested in "armed" martial arts.

Chapter 21. AN INTERVIEW WITH MASTER CHOI BOK KYU

In the west, there are many medieval martial artists. So, the ancient martial arts triggered the people here, and they saw the ancient Japanese arts, as an example, and they started to think, "Oh, don't we have our own system like that?" So, that's another reason why I emphasize some of the classical martial arts, and we don't fight with these weapons anymore, so it's more like a fun activity. They learn and maybe they get some wisdom from it, from the ancient people's wisdom, and then we can apply it in our current modern lives.

Master Choi Bok Kyu and James Theros in Amsterdam, 2011.

(End of interview)

Chapter Twenty-Two

An Interview with Grandmaster James Cook

Grandmaster James Cook is a famous martial arts practitioner in the United States who trained in Korea during the period when Korean Kung Fu was beginning to become popular in Korea and around the time that it began to spread to the United States. Grandmaster Cook was also featured in Inside Kung Fu Magazine.

Author: Where did you begin your training?

JC: In Taegeu, Korea. I had been there for one tour (military service) and I was studying Tae Kwon Do and I had been looking for a Kung Fu school. In Korea, few people realize, but, back then, about 1/8th of the population was Chinese, and in the city that I lived in, on the outskirts of the city where I was stationed at, there was a Chinese grade school and a Chinese high school; and the students that went there studied Chinese for half the day and the rest of the day they studied Korean.

There was a gentleman that I met that ran a Chinese restaurant and I informed him, we had become really good friends, and I had informed him that I was looking for a Kung Fu teacher. So he wrote a letter for me; a letter of introduction to the, at the Chinese grade school, on the roof of the grade school, the Chinese would practice every night, so I took the letter to this instructor, and it was almost like the old Kung Fu television series, where the guy kept telling me to come back next week, come back next week, come back next week.

I only had about 3 months left in the country and by the time he finally said he would accept me as a student I only had one month left, so he said, "Well, if you truly want to learn, you'll come back." Well, I got back to Fort Bragg, and after a year, I re-enlisted to go back to Korea and I was fortunate enough to get stationed in the same place.

So I walked in and he saw me and he said, "you're in class;" and, out of the class, there were approximately 20 of us; I was the only American and there was one Korean that they had allowed to come into the school.

I studied with them until the chief instructor left to go back to China; and he left a Korean student and one of his Chinese students as my private instructors who worked with me up until they graduated high school and then I went and found another school. The other school that I found, I stayed with him for about a year and a half, and then he disappeared and then I found a student of my first teacher and started studying with him and I stayed with him until I left Korea.

Author: So what year was this?

JC: We're talking about 1970 and 1971.

Author: Do you remember the name of the teacher you studied with

JC: His name was Jung Ho Ming. He was the Chinese teacher.

Author: Would you say that the training that you received was any different from the training that the Korean gentleman or the other Chinese students received?

JC: They were identical, because, see, in Korea, there's an individual, his name was Hwang Ju Hwan; and he was the president of the Korean Chinese Kung Fu Association in

Chapter 22. AN INTERVIEW WITH GRANDMASTER JAMES COOK

Korea at that Time, up in Seoul, and I had been to visit and train with him several times.

Author: So they didn't treat you any differently because you were non-Chinese?

JC: Initially they did, but because of my, I had been training since I was 10 years old, and because of my previous martial arts training they kinda looked at me as somebody kinda different; because I walked in the door understanding martial arts and they just accepted me with open arms.

I was the first black actor in Korean movies and what happened was, basically the same thing happened to me with the movie industry over there, and they couldn't believe that an American knew that much about martial arts.

Author: Speaking of your movies, are they available anywhere?

JC: I have been trying to get copies of those movies for years! I went on the internet and I found a place in Korea. One of them you can't find a copy of, but they got like clips from the movie, not even moving clips, just photographs from the movie; and the second movie I did, there was a movie house in Korea that said that I could get a copy, and I started to communicate with them, and all of a sudden, they had a Korean-American, that was like their CEO or Assistant Vice President or something, and I had emailed him several times trying to get a copy of the movie, and they wanted me to pay this much and that much and the other, and I started to smell a skunk; like I was gonna send my money over there and never see the movies.

So I'm waiting to get ahold of a friend of mine, a Korean friend of mine here in Knoxville, and, Korean is my second language, but it's been so dog-gone long since I've used it that I don't wanna screw it up, so I'm gonna get a hold of a friend of mine and see if I can get him to communicate with the movie company, and see if in fact they do actually have copies of the movie so I can get them.

I've got some 8mm film footage that I took back when we were making the movie of us on the set and doing different things.

Author: Do you remember the names of the movies you were in?

JC: The first one was called, "Dong-Poon," which means "Wind from the East." The other one was, "Massi Mat Son Karrak," which means "The Last 5 Fingers."

Author: Were you portrayed as a bad guy or a good guy?

JC: I died in both movies. I told the director, I said, "Look, can we get one where I live?" And, actually what happened was, they contracted me for a third movie that they were gonna shoot in California; but, the only problem was, and I was getting out of the service, at the beginning of 1974, and they were supposed to contact me and fly me out to California so we could do the movie, but what happened was, in Korea, you cannot get a passport unless you served in the military; and approximately two-thirds of the camera crew had never served in the military, so they had to cancel the movie in California and they changed the whole dog-gone movie and got a Korean to play my part and they did it in Korea. They called me and let me know, so I thought, "There goes my shot in the U.S."

Author: So the arts that you trained in, did they have a name?

JC: Sip Pal Gi

Chapter 22. AN INTERVIEW WITH GRANDMASTER JAMES COOK

Author: Sip Pal Gi? They called it Sip Pal Gi?

JC: Yes

Author: So, do you have any information on the origin of the actual area in China that they came from?

JC: It was so confusing, because, what was really wild was, in Korea, there were not a lot of Sip Pal Gi schools, but, the ones that they had were divided between Mantis and Bagua, and the forms were almost identical, except the biggest difference that I noticed was, I don't know if you know your Korean terminology, but, Deung San Sik (Mountain Stance), forward stance, the forward stance, your forward stance, the front foot was turned almost straight to the side. It tore your hips up, and that was the Bagua, but in the Mantis schools, both feet were at a forty-five degree angle in your forward stance.

I noticed, as a matter of fact, I was looking on youtube of you doing broadsword and that form was called, "O Ken Yan Do," and as a matter of fact, I have footage of my instructor doing it and I have footage of one of his students, who had also studied in a Bagua school, doing it; and it's an identical form but, the stances are just really weird, but different.

Author: I would love to see those. That's one of the things I'm trying to find out; nobody seems to be able to translate the word, "Ken/Kan." No one seems to know what it means.

JC: O is five. Ken is school or system. Do is the weapon.

Author: Oh, so Ken would be like Kwan, or Kan in Japanese, or Kwoon in Chinese?

JC: Right, right. Exactly.

Author: Ah, that makes sense.

JC: Yeah, it's like, the School of 5 Swords.

Author: I've seen like 6 different versions of the form. Each of them has the same movements, but in different orders, and some versions have additional movements that others do not.

JC: Right, like we have a, there's a forward roll, where once you come up out of the roll you cut under and turn in the opposite direction in a cat stance, with the forward tip next to the knee, sitting back, and, the way that the form ends, the sword is tossed up in the air and caught to the side; it's tossed up in the air with the right hand, caught with the left hand and it ends with like a long leaning-forward stance with the sword behind your back in your right hand, right above your brow, facing outward.

I've got an entire library on 8mm of two of my instructors doing all of the forms. Two of my top students have copies of those. Those are like gold to me. I rarely let those out anywhere.

We used to practice on the roof of my house, and I've got footage I took on the roof of my house in Korea.

I've got a list of all the forms written out in Korean by my instructor here; we went from the Tan Tuis, and after Tan Tuis we had So Chu Ken, which is like a bridge form that consisted of approximately 32 moves; half was on one side, half of them on the other side, and same thing on the opposite side, then we went to Baji, then we went from Baji to Sho Hu Yen, from Sho Hu Yen to Tang Lang Kwon, from Tang Lang Kwon to O Ha Kwon to Ag Ga Kwon, Ag Ga Kwon to, oh, I forgot about Jin Swee, so he's got Bo Sul, which is a basic stationery two-man form, then you've got Oo Sul, which is a single-man form that graduates to Dae Sul, which is a two-man form that moves up and down the floor.

Author: What can you tell me about the So Ho Yun form?

Chapter 22. AN INTERVIEW WITH GRANDMASTER JAMES COOK

JC: It was interpreted to us as "Small Circle Fist Form." In the form you go from the one-leg stance, jump, and turn into a rolling backfist.

Author: Yes, that's the one. So you call it the Small Circle Fist, which makes sense, because of all of the turns you do in it when you jump and turn in a circle, and then, of course, you've got the low spinning wheel kick, which is also a circle, and you've got the jump turning inside crescent kick (tornado kick), which is also a circle, so that makes a lot of sense. I've never heard it called that before.

JC: Yeah, Sun Poon Tae, the low spinning kick.

Author: That's very interesting. That certainly sheds some light on some things. Did they happen to mention what art that came from? Or any historical information on that form?

JC: I don't have any background on the form, but, like I said, everything was divided; everything that came to Korea was divided between Bagua and Mantis. They were doing the same identical forms with the stances slightly different.

One thing I noticed, because I had been to visit a couple of Bagua schools while I was stationed there, and the Bagua schools do the same identical forms but they do it slower. The Mantis schools did the forms almost twice as fast as the Bagua system.

Author: As far as the Mantis style, do you have any idea of the lineage or the branch of Mantis that it came from?

JC: Mei Hwa. Plum Flower. If I'm not mistaken it was Mei Hwa, which is Plum Flower. As far as how it came to Korea, the history is so "lost" as you might say; and when Hwang Ju Hwan, who was my Korean instructor, had taken me to Seoul to visit, and oh my god, I remember the first time I went up there; the school, it was located on the 3rd floor of this building, and there were these huge support beams in the school, and I remember, when I walked in, he was standing there; and he was throwing forearm strikes, and he's striking these poles and dust is coming out of the ceiling, and I'm looking at his forearms and I thought he had on wrist bands, but it was like his forearms were dang-near callused all the way around the arms. It was just the most incredible thing I had ever seen.

So, Jung introduces me to him, and I mean this guy had a grip; I mean you thought your hand was stuck in a vice. He was about five foot seven or, or five foot eight, a little short guy, but he was built like a tank.

He had me go through class with the entire class; there must have been about 60 or 70 of us in there, and he stuck me in front of the class and I was petrified. Then, Jung wanted to show me off, so we got up and did 2-man forms and spear and halberd and all that stuff, and he was like super impressed and I ended up taking the train up there about two or three more times to practice with his group. They were very, very welcoming and accepting.

Author: Anything else you can share with me or interesting information about the Korean martial arts?

JC: Korean systems. There's approximately 30 some systems of Tae Kwon Do and Soo Bahk Do, it's explained totally different here in the states than the way they explained it in Korea; and I remember walking down the street with my Tae Kwon Do instructor, years ago, and we were walking past this Majong house, and two guys were outside and they had grabbed each other by the lapel, and they're butting heads and kicking each other; and I said, "What in the hell are they doing?!" and he said, "Soo Bahk Do."

Soo Bahk Do consists of head-butting and kicks. If you understand Korean, the word, "Bahk;" it's a phonetic and a very descriptive language; like, if you say, the word for chicken in Korean is "Tok;" and the reason they call it tok is because when the chicken pecks at the ground is goes, "Tok, tok, tok, tok."

In Soo Bahk Do, "Bahk" is the sound that their heads make when they butt each other.

So, rice, to say the word "boil," rice is boiling, they go, "Guk Guk;" that's the sound of rice boiling and that's the word for boiling.

Author: That's great! I've studied Korean language but never had anybody explain it to me like that, but it makes perfect sense.

JC: Yeah. When I was stationed in Fort Bragg, they had a language school and you could go to after-hours language school, different schools, and I wanted to work on my Korean, and I remember the first day I walked in the class, I said, "Jin Jee Pa Soom Nikka;" which is a term that the much, much older Koreans use, which means, "Have you eaten today?" It was a term that came about during the Korean War when people were starving, and they would greet each other with, "Have you eaten today?"

If you hadn't eaten that day then they would invite you in to share whatever they had, and the teacher looked at me and she says, "Where did you learn that?" I said, "In Korea." She says, "Well, that's Korean hillbilly talk." And, I told her, I said, "Well, you understood it."

She kicked me out of the class (laughs).

Author: (laughing) So she felt insulted I guess.

JC: Well, she was from Taegu, where I was stationed at, but it's just like speaking; I took German in the 6th grade and I ended up stationed in Germany and you have a high German and that you have what they call "Swevish" (unsure of spelling), which is hillbilly German.; and the Koreans are the same way; you have high Koreans and then you have hillbilly Koreans (laughs).

I'll tell you one thing; the majority of your Sip Pal Gi teachers came from the streets. I remember Chun, my first Korean instructor. We were out at a restaurant one night and we were sitting at a table against the wall where the windows were, and there was a table behind us; and I will never forget, one of the guys behind me made a racial statement and Chun, who was about 5'5" gets up, walks over to the table and asks the guy, in Korean, "What did you say about my friend over there?"

And the guy stood up; I'd say the guy was probably 5'9" or 5'10" and he looked down at Chun and he repeated the remark. Chun took the curtain that was up against the window, pulled it over the guy's face and threw one punch, and you saw this red blotch come out of the curtain and the guy goes sliding down the wall.

Author: Oh my goodness!

JC: And he grew up in the streets of Korea and I found out, from the schools that I went to visit, that the majority of the instructors came, I mean, these guys were incredible street fighters before they got in the martial arts, and they are the smokinest, drinkinest, rowdy individuals you ever wanna meet! I mean when they throw a party, they throw a party!

(End of interview)

Chapter 22. AN INTERVIEW WITH GRANDMASTER JAMES COOK

JAMES COOK BREAKS CEMENT TILES WITH FOREHEAD

JAMES COOK DEMONSTRATES A FLYING SIDE KICK AT A SCHOOL IN KOREA

JAMES COOK WITH HIS TEACHER, HWANG JU HWAN

Chapter Twenty-Three

Interview with Grandmaster Suh Myoung Won

I found an interesting article on a Korean website about Grandmaster Suh (pronounced "saw"), in which he spoke about the art of Sip Pal Gi and mentioned several of the forms that he practiced, which were the same forms that I practice, so I took a shot and attempted to contact him by email in hopes that someone who spoke English would read it and respond.

His friend responded and graciously offered to act as intermediary between Grandmaster Suh and myself. I can read Korean and I can speak a little Korean, but not enough at the present time to be able to ask all the questions I wanted to ask, so it was necessary to have a translator available to make things simpler. I am continuing to study the Korean language so that I can better communicate with the Korean Masters and Grandmasters I meet.

The first part of this interview was done by email. I asked several basic questions and he agreed to send answers to them. After I received the answers I asked if I could call and speak to him about the art.

The second part of the interview was done by phone. Korea is exactly 12 hours ahead of my time, so early mornings seemed to work best for us. Here is the interview:

Author: Can you tell me which art these forms are from?

Grandmaster Suh: Those forms are basically from the Chinese living in Korea.

Author: Where did this art come from in China?

Grandmaster Suh: Those forms are basically concoction of Eastern China, and Taiwan.

Author: How did this art come to Korea?

Grandmaster Suh: You know that Chinese are around every corner on the planet. Korea is no exception, either. They have formed a big town in Korea as well, and started to develop their unique style of martial arts in Korea, that are quite different from the mainland China.

Author: Who were your teachers?

Grandmaster Suh: When I was young, I learned from a Korean who learned Chinese; Shaolin Quan (Sorim Kwon in Korean). Now, I am learning from Chinese, Chen Xiao Xing, Tai-ji Quan. Annually, I visit him in the Henan Province in China.

Author: Do you know what "O Ken Yan Do" means in English?

Grandmaster Suh: Basically, that must be a broken English. One who learned that word in China seemed to have a weak knowledge of Chinese. There is no such word (or a similar pronunciation) in Chinese. Therefore, I can't answer to your question, since I don't know what that exactly refers to.

Author: Can you tell me about any of the history of any of the forms from this art?

Grandmaster Suh: Some of them were originally created in themselves from the beginning, and the others were from the combination of those forms. For example, I saw Chinese practicing the So Ho Yun, when I visited China 15 years ago. But they called it Beijing Jang Quan. They explained to me that they did not know who started that style. I assume that style has been handed down from people to people without any strict guideline or direction.

Author: Do you know of Lee Duk Kang, No Soo Jun, So Sin Dang, Lim Poom Jang? What can you tell me about them?

Grandmaster Suh: I have heard of them, but never met them in real life except, Lee Duk Kang, who was reluctant to demonstrate his skills when asked. Therefore, I can't say anything about his skills, and neither can I for the rest of them. I don't want to evaluate other people who I have never met and saw their practice in real life.

Author's comments: I contacted Grandmaster Suh's friend, by phone, who acted as translator so I could ask some additional questions and see what else I could learn from him. Mr. Ho-Sung was the translator that I spoke directly to, who then asked my questions to Grandmaster Suh.

Ho-Sung (Translator); So, the Chinese characters, we got the Korean-speaking Koreans, and the Chinese we got the different pronunciation. It's quite different between those two. For example, the Chinese call the library Tu shu guan, in Korean we call it Do so ban. So, even if, I don't know who issued that kind of naming, but, basically Grandmaster Suh told me that for the names of the forms you sent him, he needs to know those exact Chinese characters or he couldn't give you the answers to those questions.

Author: What can you tell me about the broadsword form O Ken Yan Do?

Ho-Sung (Translator): Yes, yes. It's a long story. It's best I wait until you visit Korea. Then we can sit with Mr. Suh and I can translate that for you in the meeting. So, it's a long story and Mr. Suh told me that, basically, some of the forms that you mentioned in your email they come from, they have their own unique, different techniques and movements and styles, but, the others, before, they borrowed them; there was some different parts from different styles and they created their own style from those unique styles. So, they created another unique style but, basically, they borrowed the techniques from those previous styles. Each style has a long history. So, I could not put it in email because it's too long.

Author: The art that those forms come from (referring to Ag Ga Kwon, So Chu Kwon, etc...) do you call the art Sip Pal Gi?

Ho-Sung: Yes, yes. Grandmaster Suh learned Sip Pal Gi when he was in elementary school; he practiced for more than two decades. So, he practiced Sip Pal Gi because, Sip Pal Gi means "18 Different Weapons." Right? From China. So, those Sip Pal Gi, having been practiced at the Shaolin Temple; and, he converted himself to Tai Chi Quan when he was 35 or mid-thirties, and he learned from Chinese, but he was half-Chinese; we call them Chosun Cho, the North part of Korea, the northern part of North Korea, there were some Chinese; basically they are Koreans, but they come from China and

Chapter 23. INTERVIEW WITH GRANDMASTER SUH MYOUNG WON

they can speak Korean. He learned from one of them, but, when he needed to learn more in detail he visited the original place of Chen style Tai Chi Quan in Henan Province.

Ho-Sung begins speaking in Korean to Grandmaster Suh to ask him some of my questions (Since I am still working on my Korean speaking ability I figured it would go much quicker to have a native speaker ask the questions. Call to another country from a cell-phone can get expensive!)

So, regarding Sip Pal Gi, in mainland China they don't have It; so in Korea, Chinese are everywhere and we have our own Chinese town in Incheon Province. So, I believe that the first ones to arrive from mainland China, when they started to mingle with the Koreans in Korea, they, between Chinese and Koreans, they made a decision to convert those mainland techniques to 18 different weapons, so they created Sip Pal Gi.

So, Grandmaster Suh believes that Sip Pal Gi comes from the Chinese and Koreans.

Author: So, the form So Ho Yun, you said you saw them practice that in China?

Ho-Sung: Yes, he saw that.

Author: You said they called the style, "Beijing Long Fist?"

Ho-Sung: Yes, sir.

Author: What can you tell me about that form and why it is similar to the Chinese versions that I've seen, except for the movements where the practitioner does a single-leg stance and then jumps and turns into a backfist, landing in a mountain stance. The Chinese versions do not have that sequence in their versions of So Ho Yun.

Ho-Sung: He said it's very similar. He said that it does not make a big difference. He said one form, even though it is one form, when that form was handed down to many people, some people might have added their own unique form to it, but as for the style, we don't know who created it; probably one Korean or Chinese person added that jumping and this style, and that, but, Grandmaster Suh says that does not make a big difference in practicing that style. He believes they are very similar forms.

Author: Did Grandmaster Suh practice the long staff form Pal Dan Kum Bong?

Ho-Sung: He practiced it many years ago.

Author: Is that a Korean form or a Chinese form?

Ho-Sung: He said that it came from the Chinese and, even though some Koreans might call it Korean, we should say it is Chinese, because when the Chinese first arrived in Korea they transferred the forms and basically, all the roots, all those forms, come from China.

So, we should say that those styles, like Kumgang Kwon, and others, it's basically rooted from China and then Korea.

Author: Are there still a lot of schools in Korea still teaching Sip Pal Gi?

Ho-Sung: They have almost disappeared, because currently, many of them are practicing Wushu.

(End of interview)

Chapter Twenty-Four

Interview with Jin Woo Seo

While searching a Korean website, I ran across a very interesting blog page that contained several documents that were of great interest to me, including several manuals on forms that I have learned, and several that I was unfamiliar with as well. I contacted the author of the blog and he agreed to an interview on the subject of Korean Kung Fu.

Author: What is your full name?

JWS: Jin Woo Seo

Author: What is your current age?

JWS: 38 years old

Author: Where did your training in Korean Kung Fu begin?

JWS: Changwon, the city is located in South Korea
Author: How old were you when you began training?
JWS: 15 years old
Author: Who were your teachers?
JWS: My teacher name is Yoon Hang Soo
Author: What particular style of Kung Fu did you practice?
JWS: Region : Shandong, China/ Practice : Shaolin Martial Arts
Author: What can you tell me about the origins of Korean Kung Fu?
JWS: In 1940-1950, Korean Kung Fu was created by the Chinese immigrants that came over to escape the cultural revolution. The most prominent people are Lee Duk Kang (Shaolin Long Fist Style) in Seoul, Lim Poom Jang (Praying Mantis Style) in Chuncheon, Kang Kyung Bang (Praying Mantis Style) in Busan, and No Su Jeon (Bagua Style) in Incheon. In 1940-1950, the Chinese immigrants didn't teach Kung Fu to Koreans. They only taught other Chinese. In 1960, a Chinese school in Myeongdong, Seoul, a martial arts class was opened and Lim Poom Jang of Incheon was invited to teach. This is when only a select few Koreans were allowed to attend and it is believed that Korean Kung Fu began.

I know that there are also others besides Lim Poom Jang that taught and one of them is Lee Duk Kang. They admitted that they had altered the style slightly from what they have learned and passed the altered version on to their students. The basic is Dang Lang Kwon and the best techniques of Buk Beijing Long Fist were altered and brought together to make a new style called Korean-style Shaolin. In 1970 Korean Kung Fu became known in a Chinese martial arts movie.

Chapter 24. INTERVIEW WITH JIN WOO SEO

Author: What do you call the style of Kung Fu you learned?

JWS: Korean-style Shaolin

Author: Are you familiar with the long staff form "Pal Dan Kum Bong?"

JWS: I know it very well. Out of the Korean-style Shaolin long staff forms, it's the basic one to learn. There are 8 forms altogether.

Author: Are you familiar with the broadsword form "O Ken Yan Do?"

JWS: I was trained up to level 2.

Author: Are you familiar with Lee Duk Kang?

JWS: I've heard of the name. I've met him once.

Author: What do you know about him?

JWS: About 10 years ago, in Shinchon, Seoul, there was a martial arts school called Tae Eul Mun. He is one of first generation Chinese to open a school to teach and be responsible for the proper teachings of Shaolin Style. Below is a picture of Lee Duc Kang's school, Tae Eul Mun. The floor is covered in red clay which is impressive.

INSIDE OF LEE DUK KANG'S DOJANG ON THE 5TH FLOOR OF A COMMERCIAL BUILDING IN SEOUL, KOREA---READ CLAY, SALT AND WATER WERE USED TO COVER THE ENTIRE FLOOR

Author: Are you familiar with Lim Poom Jang?

JWS: I know that he has greatly influenced the Korean-style of Kung Fu in Dang Lang Kwon. This person is a high leader in Korean Kung Fu.

Author: What do you know about him?

JWS: Even though Lim Poom Jang had given a lot of influence in Korean Kung Fu, he didn't teach his altered version to his Korean students. However, one of his direct students (students that he taught personally), So Shin Dang (Chinese immigrant), opened Han Hwa Dang Lang Kwon Martial arts School and taught many students. Many first generation immigrants would alter what they have learned and teach martial arts in a slightly different style to Koreans. However, in Han Hwa Dan Lang Kwon Martial Arts School, So Shin Dang taught it exactly as he had learned from his own master. I know personally, one of his direct students and have had the chance to meet So Shin Dang once. I had the chance to hear the story about the effort he had put into martial arts. This is when I heard of an advanced kicking technique called "Wae Yang Gyu Uh".

JWS: Below is a picture of Lim Poom Jang in the position of So Deung San (Small Mountain Stance).

GRANDMASTER LIM POOM JANG PRACTICES ON ROOF TOP IN KOREA

Chapter 24. INTERVIEW WITH JIN WOO SEO

Author: Are you familiar with No Su Jun?

JWS: I know that he is the top teacher who teaches Pal Gwae "Jang" in Incheon. I don't know any details.

Author: Does Korean Kung Fu (Sip Pal Gi) come from Shaolin?

JWS: There are many sources of Sip Pal Gi. Firstly, 18 forms from a Shaolin Temple is one source for its name; Secondly, Dang Lang Kwon has a big influence in Korean Kung Fu and the techniques were taken from 18 groups of styles thus the name Lastly, "Mu Yea Do Bo Tong Ji" is a form of traditional Korean martial arts which was found recorded during the Chosun Dynasty (about 500 years ago), during the time of King Jung Jo. The techniques found here are being applied to Korean Kung Fu which is another source for the name of Sip Pal Gi.

Author: Why is the version of So Ho Yun practiced by Korean Kung Fu people different than other versions? The Korean version is the only one that I have seen that has the single-leg stance and the jump, turning back fist throughout the form. I've seen many versions but only the Korean version has these movements in it.

JSW: During the process of spreading Korean KungFu, form changes a bit from region to region. In the Chinese martial arts, there is something called a body skill (Shin Bup), it is a way to naturally connect the fixed forms. This body skill shows a little differently depending on the person's physique, there are many circumstances when the master's body skill is received by the student and changes accordingly to fit the body of the student. The truth is, after many generations, the skill is changed a lot. The martial arts KungFu takes the body skill more importantly than form so if it's not totally changed and only the partial movement is altered generally it's not worried about greatly.

Author: Do you think that the Chinese people who taught the Korean masters taught them differently to make sure that they didn't learn the "true" art?

JSW: Yes. Like Ag Ga Kwon, So Chu Kwon, Kum Gang Kwon, Mei Hwa Kwan, Kerro Kwon, Huk Ho Kwon etc...Most of it is from combining a few essential martial arts actions from Praying Mantis and Long Fist into a new form. These are stories I heard from So Shin Dang (Lim Poom Jang's student) who participated in the process of making the related forms.

(End of interview)

Chapter Twenty-Five

The Future of Korean Kung Fu

The future of Korean Kung Fu is uncertain, but, based on history (which does tend to repeat itself) I believe that it will continue to flourish around the world. I believe that, with so much access to information these days, and with books such as this one, we will begin to see some subtle shifts in the art as we currently know it.

Many of the schools in Korea have already begun implementing many of the modern Wushu/MooSul techniques and training methods into their systems. In fact, a friend of mine in Oklahoma, Grandmaster David Scott, teaches Korean Kung Fu at his school on specific nights (covering the traditional side of Kung Fu) and focuses on modern Wushu on other nights (covering the more modern approach to Kung Fu).

I believe we will see more of a shift in this general direction, and it only makes sense to do so, in order to keep up with the times. There's a reason why our military men don't use muskets anymore.

With the advent of modern technology and a shift in our general everyday lives, it is less important (and there is much less time) for the need to develop fists and arms of steel for use in mortal combat. However, there is still a place and time for such things, and I think that there will always be practitioners who are interested in doing some old-school training, as a way to connect with their ancestors, and to gain some of the remarkable skills and abilities that some of our former generations' practitioners once had.

That being said, I believe that the obvious influence that the Chinese culture has had on the martial arts world, and with the more modern influence that the United States is having on the martial arts world at large, through events like the UFC, that there will be much more blending of methods and skills from various systems of martial arts, including Kung Fu.

We are already beginning to see this in the sparring aspects of the arts. In China today, for example, Tae Kwon Do has become very popular. The Chinese have taken a lot of the Tae Kwon Do techniques and incorporated them into their Sanda/San Shou art and the Tae Kwon Do influence can easily be seen.

Many Tae Kwon Do systems are also beginning to include grappling, throwing, and striking skills from arts like Sanda, into their training as well.

And, with the advent of Youtube, it has become easier than ever to make comparisons and to use for researching techniques, skills, or entire systems or arts, in the comfort of our own homes. I suspect this will also have a huge impact on future martial arts generations. No longer are teachers able to keep techniques secretive as they did in the past. We are growing wiser as a result of all of this available information.

And there are also others like myself who are doing extensive research that is shedding light on the true history and lineage of how, where and why the various martial arts were created and transferred from location to location.

For example, is it any surprise how closely many martial arts terms sound to one another? The Korean word for "Knife Hand" is, "Soo Do," while the Japanese word for knife hand is,

Chapter 25. THE FUTURE OF KOREAN KUNG FU

"Shuto;" while the Madarin/Chinese term for knife hand is, "Shou Dao."

The term for "Martial Way" or "Martial Arts" are also very similar. In Korean, "Moo Do." In Japanese, "Bu Do." In Mandarin, "Wu Dao."

Why is this important? It's important because it shows that somewhere along the line, they all came from the same root. While the languages and written words are very different between Korean, Japanese and Chinese, many of the martial arts terms are quite similar, as illustrated by those two examples.

It's similar to comparing the Latin languages of Italian, Mexican, and Portuguese. While different, they are more similar than they are different.

Also, when comparing the Korean to Japanese, it is easy to see that the Japanese words are very strict and hard, while the Korean pronunciations are softer, but, not quite as soft as the Chinese pronunciations, which Grandmaster Na spoke about in his interview with me.

I find this very interesting, and anyone who really pays attention to this cannot deny that there is something to it. When researching history, it is important to pay attention to the smallest clues, because they can be very revealing.

It should also be interesting to note that in Korea (and I suspect in Japan as well) that many of the signs on street corners and buildings continue to have *Chinese* characters on them, and many Korean citizens are still taught how to read Chinese characters. Even one of the ways of counting, in Korean, is nearly identical in pronunciation to Cantonese/Chinese.

Since China is known as one of the oldest civilizations on earth, and since so many martial arts systems of Korea and

Japan have terms that pay homage to China (as in Tang Soo Do, which pays homage to the Chinese Tang Dynasty, and Shorin Ryu, which translates as "Shaolin System,") it might be concluded that China is indeed the birthplace of the martial arts as we know them today.

But, whatever the future holds for the Kung Fu world, and Korean Kung Fu, I hope that they will continue to practice some of the basics of the system and continue to teach some of the old-world skills to the next generation, if for no other reason than to keep history alive in some small way.

On the next page you will see a special terminology reference chart that will help demonstrate how closely-related Chinese, Korean and Japanese martial arts terminology are.

By studying this chart you will be able to see that the majority of these terms have their roots in Chinese and are still used to this day.

This is important when studying the history of the martial arts. It is very interesting to see just how many similarities there are from one language to the next and it may surprise you how similar the words actually *sound*, as if all of these words came from the same root words and were slightly modified to fit the dialect of a particular area of Asia where these words had to be used.

Along the same lines, it is also interesting to note that there are some English words that are kept as "near" English words, when spoken in Korean. A couple of examples are the words, phone, coffee, and taxi.

There are no Korean words for these particular things (and there are many others like them as well), so the Koreans simply say the same words, but they slightly change them to fit the Korean language.

Chapter Twenty-Six

Reference Chart & Korean Alphabet

Terminology Reference Chart

English Analysis	Mandarin Fenjie	Cantonese Fen Gai	Korean Boon Hae	Japanese Bunkai	Chinese Characters 分解	Korean Hangul 분해	Japanese Kanji 分解
Attention	Jí Zhōng	Zaap Zung	Cha Ryut	Keiot Suke	集中	차렷	気を付け
Basic/Elementary	Jiben	Gei Bun	Kibon	Kihon	基本的	기본	基本
Begin/Start	Kai Shir	Hoy Chi	Shijak	Hajime	开始	시작	始
Belt/Sash	Dai	Taai	Dee	Obi	带	띠	帯
Block	Shou Dao	Kwa, Sao	Mahk Ki	Uke	收到	막기	受け
Bow	Bao Quan	Kow Tow	Kyung Net/Kyung Yet	Rei	敬禮, 丽	경례	礼
Broadsword	Dao	Dau	Do	To	刀	도	ナイフ
Cheers	Gam Be	Gom Bui	Kon Bae	Kan Pai	乾杯	건배	乾杯
Double	Shuang	Cern	Ssang	Daburu	雙	쌍	ダブル
Empty Mind	Wu Shin/Xin	Mou Sum	Mu Shim	Bu Shin	無心	무심	無心
Energy	Qi/Chi	Chi	Ki	Ki	氣	기	気
Energy Center/Diapragm	Dan Tien	Dan Tim	Dan Jun	Tan Den	丹田	단전	陰毛
Fighting/Sparring	Shou, Shou, Sanda	San Sao	Derrien, Gyorugi	Kumite	搏, 對練, 散打, 搏击	대련, 겨루기	組手
Fist	Quan/Chuan	Kuen/Kune, kyun	Kwon	Ken	拳	권	拳
Fist Law	Chuan Fa/Quan Fa	Keun Faht	Kwon Bup	Kenpo/Kempo	拳法	권법	拳法
Foot	Jiao	Jok, Geuk	Bal	Ashi	脚	발	足
Form/Pattern	Tao Lu	Tou Lou, Sik	Touro/Pooomse/Hyung/Tul	Kata	套路	투로, 형	型
Foundation, Elementary	Chuji	Gay cho	Ki Cho	Ki Sho	基礎, 初級	기초	基礎
Grade Below Black Belt	Ji	Kap	Gup	Kyu	級, 类	급	級
Grand Ultimate Fist	Taiji Quan/Tai Chi Quan/Chuan	Tai Gik Kune	Tae Geuk Kwon	Tai Kyoku Ken	太极拳	태극권	太極拳

311

Korean Kung Fu: The Chinese Connection

English Analysis	Mandarin Fenjie	Cantonese Fen Gai	Korean Boon Hae	Japanese Bunkai	Chinese Characters 分解	Korean Hangul 분해	Japanese Kanji 分解
Hand	Shou	Sau/Soo	Son, Su	Te	手	손, 수	手
Horse Stance	Ma Bu	Ma Bo	Ki Ma Ja Sae/Sik	Kibadachi	騎馬立ち, 騎馬 姿勢	기마 자세	騎馬立
Kicking	Tui	Toy, Ti/Tek	Tae	Geri	踢	태	蹴り
Knife Hand	Shou Dao	Sou Dau	Sudo	Shuto	手刀	수도	手刀
Level/Degree	Duan	Dyun	Dan	Dan	段	단	段
Little Forest	Shaolin	Sil Lum/Siu Lum	Sorim	Shorin	少林	소림	少林
Martial Way	Wu Dao	Mo Dou	Mu Do	Bu Do	武道	무도	武道
Master	Shi Fan		Sabum	Kyoshi	師範	사범	教師
Meditation	Ming Xian	Meng Sun	Myong Sang, Moog Nyum	Meiso	冥想	명상, 묵념	瞑想
Military/War	Wu	Mo	Mu	Bu	武	무	武
Opposites/Balance	Yin Yang	Yuen Yeung	Um Yang	In Yo	陰 陽	음양	陰陽
Partner Practice	Dui Da, Duilian	Doylin	Dae Ta, Derrien, Dalyun	Yaku SoKu Kumite, Taiku	對打, 對練	대타, 대련, 달련	対句, 約束 組手
Punching/Striking/Attacking	Gongji	Gung Gik	Kong Kyuk	Tsuki	攻擊, 推力技术	공격	攻 擊技, 突き技
Spear	Chiang	Coeng	Chang	Yari	槍	창	槍
Spirit Yell/Battle Cry	Chi He/Qi He	Hei Hop	Ki Hap	Ki Ai	氣合	기합	気 合
Springy Legs	Tan Tui	Dan Tuy, Dam Doi	Tan Tei		潭腿, 彈腿	단 퇴, 담퇴	
Staff	Bang, Gun/Gwen	Gwan	Bong	Bo	棒, 棍	봉	棒
Stance	Zi Shi, Bu	Sik, Bo	Ja Sae	Dachi	式, 姿勢, 步, 開始	자세	立ち
Style/Association	Liu	Lau	Yoo	Ryu	流, 风格	류	流
Sword (straight or Samurai-style)	Jian	Gim	Kum	Ken	劍, 剑	검	劍
System/Style	Pai	Pai	Kwan	Kan	派, 馆	관	館, 派閥,
Teacher	Si Fan, Lau Si	Si Fu	Sabum	Shihan	師範, 老師	사범	先 生
Teacher	Shifu/Sherfu	Sifu	Sabum	Sensei/Shi Chi	師父, 師範	사범	先生
The Discipline/Skill	Kung Fu/Gung Fu	Gong Fu	Kung Hu/Koong Bu/Goong Bu	Ken Po, Kan Fu	功夫	쿵후, 쿵부, 궁부	功夫

Chapter 26. REFERENCE CHART AND KOREAN ALPHABET

English Analysis	Mandarin Fenjie	Cantonese Fen Gai	Korean Boon Hae	Japanese Bunkai	Chinese Characters 分解	Korean Hangul 분해	Japanese Kanji 分解
The Way of Coordinated Power	He Chi Dao	Hap Hei Dou	Hapkido	Aikido	合氣道	합기도	合気道
The Way of Hand & Foot	Tai Chuan Dao	Ti Keun Dou	Tae Kwon Do	Tai Ken Do	跆拳道	태권도	テコンドー
Training Hall/ School	DaoChang, Guan	Kwoon	Dojang	Dojo	道場	도장	道場
Uniform	Kung Fu Eefu	Sam	Do Bok	Do Gi	道服	도복	着
War Art	Wushu	Mo Sut	Mu Sul	Bu Jitsu	武術	무술	武術
Way	Dao	Dou	Do	Do	道	도	道
Weapons	Bingqi	Bing Hey	Byung Gi	Bu ki	兵器, 武器	병기	武器

So, in Korea, they say, "Pone" for Phone. Since the Korean language has no "f" sound, they substitute the "f" sound with a "p" sound instead. So, when they say the word coffee, they call it, "Coppee" (similar to "copy,") and when they say the word "taxi," they simply say "Tehk-see" (it sounds nearly identical, but there is still a slight "Korean" dialect to it.)

So, why is this important? It is important because I believe that the fact that so many Korean and Japanese martial arts terms sound like Chinese terms, and China is much older than either Japan or Korea, this helps to prove that the martial arts of Korea and Japan had their roots in Chinese martial arts first.

Korean Hangul

I believe it is valuable for all Korean martial artists to learn to read, write and speak Korean. Learning how to do so will greatly enhance your understanding of the art that you are studying and to help clean up some of the mispronunciations in the Korean martial arts world.

Consonants	ㅏ (a)	ㅑ (ya)	ㅓ (o)	ㅕ (yo)	ㅗ (oh)	ㅛ (yo)	ㅜ (ow)	ㅠ (you)	ㅡ (er)	ㅣ (ee)
ㄱ (G)	가	갸	거	겨	고	교	구	규	그	기
ㄴ (N)	나	냐	너	녀	노	뇨	누	뉴	느	니
ㄷ (D)	다	댜	더	뎌	도	됴	두	듀	드	디
ㄹ (R/L)	라	랴	러	려	로	료	루	류	르	리
ㅁ (M)	마	먀	머	며	모	묘	무	뮤	므	미
ㅂ (B)	바	뱌	버	벼	보	뵤	부	뷰	브	비
ㅅ (S)	사	샤	서	셔	소	쇼	수	슈	스	시
ㅇ Silent	아	야	어	여	오	요	우	유	으	이
ㅈ (J)	자	쟈	저	져	조	죠	주	쥬	즈	지
ㅊ (CH)	차	챠	처	쳐	초	쵸	추	츄	츠	치
ㅋ (K)	카	캬	커	켜	코	쿄	쿠	큐	크	키
ㅌ (T)	타	탸	터	텨	토	툐	투	튜	트	티
ㅍ (P)	파	퍄	퍼	펴	포	표	푸	퓨	프	피
ㅎ (H)	하	햐	허	혀	호	효	후	휴	흐	히

This simplistic chart of the Korean language, known as *Hangul* shows the primary consonant characters down the left side and the primary vowels across the top. Upon looking at the chart you can then follow from left to right from the top. The first *consonant* shown is "ㄱ" which is pronounced as a hard "g" or "k" sound (depending on which vowel comes after it or before it.)

Chapter 26. REFERENCE CHART AND KOREAN ALPHABET

The first *vowel is* "ㅏ" which is pronounced as, "Ah," so the two characters, combined, create, "가" (which makes the sound, "Ga" or "Ka"), so if you take the 3rd consonant (ㄷ), which is pronounced as a hard "d" or "t" (usually somewhere in between those two sounds) and we add the 5th vowel over from the left (ㅗ) which is pronounced as, "Oh" and combine them, we come up with "도" which makes the sound, "Dough" as in "Tae Kwon Do (태권도)" or "Do Bok (도복)."

The Korean alphabet is something that all Korean martial artists should learn as it will help to correct a lot of improperly pronounced words that are used by us Americans (including the often-mispronounced Do Bok).

Many students, and masters, pronounce it "Do Bock," when referring to the martial arts uniform.

If you read the Korean characters (도복) you will see that the "o's" are long o's and the "k" sound at the end is not to be fully aspirated, rather, cut short, almost like the sound of a hard "g" (as in the word gun).

Traditional Korean clothing is called Han Bok (한복), pronounced, Hahn Boke." The word Han means "Korean", as in Hangul (the written language of Korea), and Bok (복) means "clothing."

Do (도) means, "The Way," so, literally translated; a Do Bok (도복) is "Clothing of the Way."

There is also a *generally-accepted* method of writing the Korean language in English.

Typically, the words Tae Kwon Do or Hap Ki Do are spelled as written here, but it would not actually be *completely* incorrect to write them as Teh Kwan Do or Hab Kee Do, as long as the pronunciation was correct.

You'll not usually see strange spellings of those arts though, except by a person who has never trained in those arts.

They are usually written in English, respectively, as Tae Kwon Do (or Taekwondo, which is often used when describing the WTF sports-oriented version, versus the more traditional style of Tae Kwon Do---with spaces between syllables) and Hapkido (or Hap Ki Do)

Again, both of the names of these arts are often butchered by us Americans.

Many people (even high ranking American masters) often call Tae Kwon Do "Tai" or "Tie" Kwon Do, and Hap (as in Hapkido,(합)기도) is often pronounced "Happ" (as in happen), which is also incorrect. Hapkido's proper pronunciation is "Hop"Kido.

One look at the Korean alphabet will clear these things up.

I believe this is very important for any serious student.

If one were to become a doctor, one would be expected to know the names of the different tools used in their practice, such as a stethoscope, for instance, and there is only one way to pronounce it.

Pronouncing it "stetha-scop" (without the long "o" sound) would indicate a lack of education on the part of that doctor and may cost him his job or at the very least he would have patients that would question his validity as a real doctor.

Think about that for a moment.

There are far too many traditional martial artists who don't feel the need to learn the correct pronunciation of the terminology words used in their system.

It shows a sense of pride and is impressive to a person of Korean decent to hear their language spoken properly; just

Chapter 26. REFERENCE CHART AND KOREAN ALPHABET

as Americans, we appreciate when a foreign person learns to speak our language with proper pronunciation.

The Korean language is said to be the world's most scientifically sound written language, due to its simplicity. It was created by King Sejong in 1443 and has been left virtually unchanged since its creation.

Hangul letters are grouped into blocks, such as 한 *Han*, each of which transcribes a syllable. That is, although the syllable 한 Han may look like a single character, it is actually composed of three letters: ㅎ h, ㅏ a, and ㄴ n.

Each syllabic block consists of two to five letters, including at least one consonant and one vowel. These blocks are then arranged horizontally from left to right or vertically from top to bottom.

It will take a little time to get used to because you must memorize the sounds that each of the characters makes, but it will be worth it and in very little time, you'll be reading, writing and speaking authentic Korean and you might even understand what your master is saying about you to his friends. (wink, wink!)

Additionally, it can be very useful to learn how to count in Korean. The majority of Korean-operated martial arts schools include basic Korean counting in their programs.

There are two methods of counting in the Korean language. The first is the purely Korean system, and is the one commonly used in many martial arts schools.

The second method (and much older method) is what is known as the Sino-Korean system. Sino comes from Latin and Greek and was used in reference to all things Chinese, so, *once again*, we see Korea's connection to China. This particular

Korean Kung Fu: The Chinese Connection

counting system is generally used when counting "sets" of something, such as hours of the day or, in martial arts, forms that come from the same set, such as Tae Geuk Il Jang or Palgwe Yi Jang. In both the Tae Geuk and Palgwe sets there are 8 "chapters" (which is what the word, *Jang* means) and the numbers are used to describe which "chapter" from the set that they are from.

Below is a chart showing the Korean, Sino-Korean, Mandarin and Cantonese numbers. I have used phonetic spellings to better illustrate their proper pronunciations. There are generally-accepted English spellings of both Korean and Chinese words, but I find them to be a little misleading when it comes to accurately pronouncing them, so, rather than writing the words as one might see them elsewhere, I have attempted to make it easy to pronounce the words as accurately as possible. Interestingly, the Chinese characters are identical in Mandarin and Cantonese, but they are *pronounced* very differently in each respective language.

Number	Korean	Hangul	Sino-Korean	Hangul	Mandarin	Cantonese	Chinese
1	Hana	하나	Il	일	Ee	Yāt	一
2	Dool	둘	Yi	이	Ar	Yi	二
3	Set	셋	Sahm	삼	San	Sāam	三
4	Net	넷	Sah	사	Suh	Sei	四
5	Dah-Sawt	다섯	Oh	오	Wu	Ng	五
6	Yaw-Sawt	여섯	Yook	육	Lee-Oo	Luhk	六
7	Il-Gop	일곱	Chil	칠	Chi	Chāt	七
8	Yaw-Dawl	여덟	Pal	팔	Ba	Baat	八
9	Ah-Hope	아홉	Koo	구	Jee-Ew	Gáu	九
10	Yoewl	열	Ship	십	Sher	Sahp	十

Chapter 26. REFERENCE CHART AND KOREAN ALPHABET

What I find quite interesting is that the Sino-Korean number system sounds much closer to the Cantonese pronunciations of the numbers, rather than the mandarin (with a couple of obvious exceptions), as do many of the martial arts terminology words used in Korean martial arts, particularly the older systems, such as Tang Soo Do.

It is also interesting to note that the newer ITF and WTF Tae Kwon Do systems chose to use completely different terminology to describe their movements (blocks, strikes, kicks, stances, etc...) This, I suspect, was part of making their art purely Korean; and who could blame them after what they went through during their occupation by the Japanese government in World War II. The reason I bring this up is because when I began my training we used very different Korean terminology for the words, "Strike," "Stance," "Fighting," etc...

For example, in our program, we call a middle punch a, Choong Dan Kon Kyuk (which means a middle "attack") versus a Momtong Chigi (as used by most Tae Kwon Do systems today) which is a middle punch/strike to the body, and we call a front stance Chungul Ja Sae, while others call it an Ahp Sogi.

I have noticed that schools who teach Tang Soo Do (or older versions of Tae Kwon Do) use the older terms that are more closely-related to the Chinese terms, whereas the newer styles of TKD use a completely different set of terminology words to describe the same movements.

If your teacher uses terms like Ja Sae (stance), Kon Kyuk (punch/attack) and Derrien Ja Sae (fighting stance) then your background is likely more of a traditional nature. If your master uses terms like Sogi (stance), Chigi/Chireugi (strike, punch) or Gyorugi Sogi (fighting stance) then you are likely part of a more modern version of Tae Kwon Do or Tang Soo Do- Just an interesting little piece of information for you.

Be sure to return back to the terminology chart and see how closely many of the Korean terms relate with the Cantonese terms, which again, is strange, because Cantonese is spoken primarily in *Southern China*, which is further away from Korea than Northern China is. One would expect that there would be a closer similarity to Mandarin to Korean than to Cantonese, as appears to be the case.

In America, we often study Latin to find the root-words of many words used in the English language.

I have to wonder what the Cantonese connection is and why it seems to have such a close sound to many of the Korean numbers and martial arts language used in the Korean language, rather than Mandarin. There are a many similarities to Mandarin as well, though, so the mystery remains. Maybe I'll have answers in another book in the future.

CONCLUSION

The conclusions about the art of Korean Kung Fu are that the art is an eclectic system that has influences of Northern Shaolin Long Fist, blended with Northern Praying Mantis, and Bagua, and that the art came to Korea by way of Shandong, China, Taiwan, and Manchuria (by the respective masters who emigrated to Korea in the early 1900's.)

The art was then further developed in South Korea, by the masters who brought their respective systems from their homelands. They worked together as a team of friends and associates and shared their knowledge between each other to further develop the system as we know it today.

The art was not officially shared with the Korean masters until the 1960's, when a few of the Chinese masters began teaching it to the Koreans.

Some of the Korean masters favored specific elements of one particular art and gravitated more towards teaching that particular style's essence (flavor) and slightly modifed the forms taught to them, putting more emphasis on either the Long Fist elements or the Praying Mantis elements, even though the forms are nearly identical.

There is also a very popular style of pure Praying Mantis Kung Fu that is prevalent in Korea, that has also greatly influence the art of Korean Kung Fu, and some systems actually teach this Praying Mantis system along with Sip Pal Gi.

According to my sources, the style of Praying Mantis taught in Korea is largely the Mei Hua Tang Lang/Nang system. I have learned several of the forms form this system, but I will say that the Korean versions are a bit more simplified than the Chinese version of the same system.

For example, the 3 Mei Hwa forms Mei Hwa of Mei Hwa Tang Lang Quan (Mei Hwa Kwon, Mei Hwa Soo Kwon and Mei Hwa Ro Kwon) are certainly identifiable as such, but, when compared to the Chinese versions, the Chinese versions have a stronger emphasis on footwork, and there are additional hand techniques that are not included in the Korean versions.

MEI HWA KWON BOOK SERIES BY SO SIN DANG

The Korean system of Mei Hwa Tang Lang Quan was largely taught in Korea by Grandmaster So Shin Dang, from Taiwan, who has written several books in Korean on those forms, as well as several other forms.

One interesting fact that I discovered when reading his book on Jin Gang Quan (Kum Gang Kwon) is that he shows the very same form in his book that is taught in most Sip Pal Gi schools, even though it comes from a pure Praying Mantis system.

This is an example of borrowing a form from a particular

CONCLUSION

art (Praying Mantis, in this case) and then either leaving the mantis influence intact, or slowing it down and adding more Long Fist elements to it, by changing some of the hand and foot positions from mantis hooks/catches, to simple closed fists or modifying a movement so that it is a bit less circular, to better fit in with the other forms in the system.

Additionally, the 7-Star Praying Mantis (Chil Sung Tang Nang Kwon) system is also largely taught in Korea, so there are some elements and forms from that system that have found their way into Sip Pal Gi as well.

It may even be considered that Sip Pal Gi is one of the world's first "mixed martial arts" styles, since it has borrowed concepts from several systems and condensed them into a single "style" for lack of a better term.

And, one must not forget, it was also around this same time period that Bruce Lee was combining elements and techniques from "26" different arts to develop the art that he later called "Jeet Kune Do" (Way of the Intercepting Fist).

Very few things on this earth are "pure" anymore. Various cultures have continually adopted pieces of one another's cultures for as long as humans have been on the earth.

So, where does the "Shaolin" connection come in? The answer is twofold; firstly, the Long Fist techniques are taken directly from Northern Shaolin Long Fist Kung Fu, and secondly, Northern Praying Mantis Kung Fu was created by Grandmaster Wang Lang, who studied at the Shaolin Temple and created the art of Praying Mantis Kung Fu during his time at the temple. We sometimes refer to our art as "Original Shaolin Kung Fu" and this is the reason for it. In recent years it has also been referred to as "Korean Shaolin Kung Fu."

This is because the art originally came from the Shaolin Temple in China and was passed on to the the Koreans, where it was slightly modified and developed since that time, around the mid 1950's---just like most other Korean arts were being developed around that time. The arts of Tang Soo Do, Tae Kwon Do, Hapkido, Kumdo, Hwa Rang Do, Kuk Sool Won, (etc.) were all in their beginning stages of development at around the same time period, due to the Japanese occupation, so Sip Pal Gi was among those arts that were developed around that time, as well.

At that time, the Koreans were very busy throwing off the shackles of oppression by the Japanese and it was a period of renaissance for the Koreans, so they were very excited about developing their own arts and culture, and they were slightly modifying each of the arts that had been imported from China, as well as Japan.

This is why, in virtually every *Korean* martial art, we see close similarities to Japanese and Chinese arts, with subtle differences, to make their arts more Korean. As time passed, the Korean masters began to slowly modify things each year, adding things and discarding others until they brought the arts to the stages that they are in today. Even as late as the year 2000, Grandmaster Choi Hong Hi innovated in his art, by including the now-standard "sine wave" pattern that is practiced by many ITF schools today.

There will likely be further development by other Korean arts in the very near future. So, all that this means is that the martial arts have been continually developing and evolving- pretty much since the time of their creation.

One thing that many martial artists may not be aware of

is that the Shaolin Temple and the monks who trained there learned a huge variety of martial arts styles. The Abbot of the Shaolin Temple (the great monk Fu Ju) invited 18 different martial arts masters to visit the monastery to teach the monks a variety of skills and techniques to enhance their abilities (sounds a bit like today's MMA, if you ask me) and they learned a great variety of skills. Grandmaster Wang Lang was one of these 18 masters who were invited to teach.

So, basically all martial arts have evloved over the years, in an attempt to eliminate the weaknesses in their art and by adding skills and techniques from other martial arts to strengthen their arts' effectiveness.

In today's martial arts landscape, a great majority of systems have added grappling skills and weapons skills to their arts to make them more complete.

Many Tae Kwon Do schools also teach the art of Hapkido in their curriculum. Hapkido is a separate art, and a very comprehensive one at that, but it fits nicely in with the Tae Kwon Do curriculum and enhances the practitioner's self-defense abilities, and many of today's Japanese, Okinawan, and Chinese stylists have added some of the footwork, kicks, and fighting skills of Tae Kwon Do into their curriculum for the same reason.

Another interesting bit of information that many may be unaware of, is that a good deal of the Chinese Kung Fu movies that were filmed in the 1970's and early 1980's actually starred *Korean* masters who were dressed in Chinese clothing, and many of these Koreans were very famous for their martial arts skills on the big screen in Asia.

Two of the more notable Koreans to star in these Kung Fu movies were Hwang Jang Lee (also known as the "Silver

Fox") and Kim Tai Jung, who doubled as "Bruce Lee" in many movies, including the cheesy 80's cult hit "No Retreat, No Surrender" with Jean-Claude Van Damme.

ABOVE:
HWANG JANG LEE (AKA "THE SILVER FOX)

AT RIGHT:
HWANG JU HWAN AND STUDENT KIM TAI JUNG, WHO PORTRAYED BRUCE LEE IN MANY HONG KONG MOVIES AND IN "NO RETREAT, NO SURRENDER" WITH JEAN-CLAUDE VAN DAMME

In closing, I'd like to reiterate that the information contained in this book and ideas presented are only educated guesses at best, as it is virtually impossible to prove any of it, until we actually invent a machine that will allow us to travel back in time to properly document the true origins of the martial arts.

I make no claims of knowing all there is to know about the history of the martial arts, and each year I learn a little more, which is one of the reasons I continue my studies.

I find history fascinating, and it drives me to continue to search for information and knowledge. In this book I have only presented my personal opinions (melded with the information that I have gleaned from my research and from my trusted and valued sources), based on my findings through my studies and travels.

I believe that all martial arts are good and all of them serve a purpose. Much like we all have different tastes when it comes to the car we drive, the home we live in, the type of food we enjoy, etc....

I also believe that all martial arts have value and should never be negatively spoken about, in regards to which art is better, more practical, more realistic, etc....

There have always been politics in the martial arts (and probably always will be).

Some systems (or schools) of martial arts focus more on straight-forward, no-nonsense techniques that have been proven on the street; but this shouldn't discount a school that uses the martial arts as a vehicle for personal and character development.

And there are other schools that teach their martial art as more of a *sport*, where the majority of the training is geared towards competitions and sparring than on self-defense skills. I find nothing wrong with this approach, either; and there are also martial arts schools who teach their art more for *fitness* purposes.

The martial arts are as diverse as most other things are. In the world of automobiles some people use their vehicle to get them from point a to point b, while others use their vehicle to attract attention from others or as a status symbol. Still, others may use their vehicle to aid them in their work (construction or painting companies come to mind). While others collect and trade vehicles as a source of income or a source of personal enjoyment.

When it comes to the martial arts, for some reason, there are people who don't understand that this same concept applies to martial arts training, too.

There are countless people who talk down about martial arts training that is different from their own for a variety of reasons. You can recognize these folks when you hear them talking about the ineffectiveness of certain techniques in the martial arts.

It is important to keep a couple of things in mind regarding this line of thinking. Firstly, some techniques in a martial art are used to help train a specific *skill* or *attribute* (such as strength or coordination), which might apply to the horse stance, the cat stance, or chambering one's arm by the waist during a form, although there are certainly plausible self-defense applications for those as well.

Regarding the horse stance, for example, one may not ever fight using that stance, but, then again, in a grappling situation, one might find themselves in a position that looks and feels pretty close to one. In regards to chambering the arm by the waist, what if that technique is actually more than it appears at first. If that fist by the waist was a pull to an opponent's garment or limb then it would make more sense.

So, what may at first look like it has no value may actually have more value than originally thought. It's important to keep an open mind as a martial artist and remember that the masters of yesteryear knew what they were doing when they created the various arts.

Something else to keep in mind is that the more complex a technique is the more time and training will be needed to

CONCLUSION

make it work in a real encounter; and sometimes, the situation has to be *just* right for some techniques to work.

That is one of the reasons that there are so many different self-defense techniques in any one martial art. Very few things work 100% of the time, but, under the right circumstances, virtually anything could work.

In the case with Chinese Kung Fu, what must be taken into consideration is that the techniques were not meant for competition. They were designed with the purpose of strengthening one's body and mind and giving the practitioner the ability to protect him/herself and or their family and community.

I'll be the first to admit that there are a lot of very weak-looking martial artists, Kung Fu practitioners included. One should not judge a martial art by the practitioners who only *half-heartedly* train. You could take these very same people and teach them the world's most deadly martial art and they would make it look impractical.

But, you can also take a person who wants to train sincerely and seriously and then, whatever fighting system they practiced would look practical and would work in real situations.

It always boils down to the individual person. All fighting arts require power; even Tai Chi. Without power there is little chance of victory in a fight.

Learning where to strike an opponent is important, learning when to strike an opponent is important, learning what to strike an opponent *with* is important as well, but, without a certain amount of speed, power, intensity and coordination, there will be no victory.

In today's martial arts landscape there are many choices, from boxing to wrestling to MMA to Tae Kwon Do or Karate, from Judo to Jiujitsu or Brazillian Jiujitsu to Kung Fu or Tai Chi or even martial arts for toddlers.

They all have something to offer and all of them serve a purpose.

In regards to the more sports-oriented martial arts, I look at it this way, football is a sport, too, but if a football player (who learns to throw, tackle and hit) uses some of what they learned in the sport of football in a real fight, it's easy to see how some of it could be valuable. Same with boxing. Even though a boxer only uses his hands, if he learns how to use his hands with the effectiveness of a world-class boxer then he will have an absolute advantage over someone without those skills.

Bruce Lee once said, "I don't fear the man who has practiced 10,000 kicks one time. I fear the man who has practiced one kick 10,000 times."

So, if a martial artist learns a thousand techniques he or she will still likely focus on only a handful of techniques that work for them and that fit their body type, coordination and psychological preferences.

Since everyone is different, there are a good variety of techniques to choose from, and, until we have trained with various techniques and skills for some time, we don't know which techniques are best suited for us.

There is room for everyone in the martial arts. My personal opinion on the current state of the world of martial arts, though, is that I feel many people have gotten away from the traditional side of the martial arts; mainly due to a lot of the political rigmarole that we find so common on the internet and many of the trade publications these days, along with the growing popularity of mixed martial arts competitions on television.

When MMA first came on the scene it was an exciting thing to watch, as they pitted one style against another. The lesson eventually learned was that there was no *style* better than another. It always came down to the *person* who used the style.

Eventually, though, the competitors learned that they needed to improve their grappling skills if they intended on doing well in those competitions, and the grapplers realized that they needed to work on their punching and kicking skills.

The sport continues to evolve as techniques are added to their repertoire each year, and some day we will most likely see a complete system developed from techniques that worked in the cage. Funny thing is, they will be simply reinventing the wheel.

How do you think the existing martial arts systems came into being in the first place?

At the time of the writing of this book we are witnessing the return to traditional martial arts training, including many of today's MMA fighters who are looking to increase their skills and knowledge by becoming students at traditional schools of martial arts. So, in that regard, it's good to see the renewed interest in the traditional arts.

Who's to say which art is the best and which art is being practiced "properly?" Ask any practitioner of Jeet Kune Do who is right? Ask someone who practices WTF Tae Kwon Do about the training methods of an ITF Tae Kwon Do practitioner and you are in for one long-winded argument on which one is better, or more pure, etc....

You will find the same thing with Kenpo Karate, particularly after Ed Parker passed away. This is simply human nature. Religions work this way, sports work this way, chiropractic skills work this way, Eastern versus Western medicine works this way, business works this way. It's simply human nature at work.

Something else to keep in mind is that every master adds his/her own uniqueness to any martial art. Consider people like Gichin Funakoshi (creator of Shotokan Karate), General Choi Hong Hi (creator of ITF Tae Kwon Do), Jigoro Kano (creator of Judo), Bruce Lee (creator of Jeet Kune Do), and others who have gone on to make alterations to the arts that they were taught.

While there have been attempts to standardize certain arts, there is no denying that all arts have been adapted over time by the instructor to best fit what he/she felt most important. Changes to the way a technique is executed (a low block, for instance) have been happening as long as the techniques have been around.

I've seen people from the exact same system (mine included) who perform a recognizable form but perform nearly everything differently; different emphasis on footwork, speed, power, intensity levels, different strikes than the ones we use in that same section of the form, different blocks, kicks, etc.... Yet, I still recognize the form.

I've seen this phenomenon in just about every martial art that I've ever studied or seen. You have probably seen it, too. Do a search on YouTube for a form or technique from the system you are studying and you're likely to see multiple versions of it and to hear varying opinions about different aspects of the form or technique.

I've seen the exact same technique taught one way (as the "correct way") in one school, and been told that that way is "incorrect" at another school.

So, who is right? I believe all of them are right. When in

Rome, do as the Romans do. I believe that every martial artist should find what works best for them and use that. I have no doubt that my own students will one day teach techniques and forms differently than I taught them, if they practice long and hard enough and develop the passion to teach, as I have.

This is only natural. I also believe that my students will retain some of the flavor of the form that I taught them. This, too, is only natural. So it is with all martial arts, I suspect.

I myself have made small changes to the art that I teach, particularly due to the fact that I have trained in this Kung Fu system with 3 separate teachers, each with their own beliefs about what is important and which way is the right way to do it. I have taken all of their ideas and concepts and applied them at different places in my training.

I have also trained with various Chinese masters who have undoubtedly influenced me as well in regards to my personal interpretation of my art. All arts are good and all arts have room for personalization by the practitioner; particularly after that practitioner has spent 20 to 30 years in learning and practicing their art.

Keep an open mind when learning a martial art and have faith in your teacher. Unless you trust your instructor it will be virtually impossible to excel in your learning.

In the traditional martial arts, part of mastering the art is your experience in teaching and working with others and learning from that experience. There's an old saying, "When one teaches two learn." This is how a master instructor is created.

Through the teaching process we often learn things that we would never learn otherwise. Having to relay information to another person strengthens our own understanding of whatever we are sharing or teaching.

This should not be overlooked. Most of the world's most gifted martial artists are also some of the most giving teachers. The more time you spend working with others and teaching, the more you will learn.

The famous Chinese philosopher Lao Tzu said, "Wisdom is knowing others. Enlightenment is knowing yourself."

One gains wisdom through working with others and teaching others. The experience allows the teacher to begin to see the commonalities that human beings have with one another and their patterns and thought-processes begin to reveal themselves.

The continued training in traditional martial arts, including working with others, will help reveal specific insights to the practitioner that will only occur through the trials and tribulations associated with training.

Each time we have a struggle we learn something about ourselves. We may either learn that we are stronger and more capable than we originally thought, or we may learn that we have fears and doubts that we didn't realize were hiding just under the surface.

With continued training in the martial arts we come to know others and, more importantly, we come to know ourselves; and we have the ability to make improvements to our character where needed while empowering us with the ability to help others learn and grow as well. It is our responsibility as human beings to pass on and share our findings with those who come after us.

I sincerely hope that this book helps you find some wisdom and enlightenment and I wish you success. Expect some setbacks and failures along your journey and keep this final thought in the forefront of your mind at all times, "It's not the destination, it's the journey."

Acknowledgements

I'd like to thank the following individuals for their friendship and support over the years. Without these people this book would not have been possible.

Firstly, thanks, for igniting my passion for Kung Fu and for the 20 years of wonderful instruction goes to my original master, Grandmaster Young Pyo Choi. I watched you for years and did my best to emulate your every move. Anytime you performed I was right there at your feet with my video camera because I didn't want to miss anything. And, for all of the late-night talks we had about martial arts and about life, on the way to and from tournaments and at your office. Thank you, sir. You changed my life.

Secondly, to Grandmaster Joon Pyo Choi for inspiring me at so many promotion tests, tournaments and demonstrations, with your words of wisdom and your input on my training. You once told a large group of students at a summer camp that I had "strong basics" and you have no idea just how much that simple statement affected me and pushed me to work harder to gain your respect.

Thirdly, to Yorgo Lorandos and Rey Santiago, who basically took me under their wing at Grandmaster Byong Yil Choi's school and supported me during a very difficult transitional time in my life.

Fourthly, special thanks goes out to Master Henry Murphy for spending the day making my brain hurt with all of the historical information on the pioneers of the Korean martial arts and for introducing me to Grandmaster Hi Na.

Next, I'd like to say thank you to Grandmaster Hi Seup Na. I have treasured our relationship and I can't thank you enough for the years of friendship and for your unbelievable generosity in sharing your knowledge with me over the years. You are an incredible martial arts master and I wish you all the success life has to offer. You helped me complete my journey in Kung Fu and in so many other ways as well.

To my good friend, Master Kenny Perez, I thank you for allowing me to train with you and to stay at your home so many times with your wonderful family. Thank you for openly sharing your knowledge and friendship with me and for helping me to put some real Chinese-flavor into my training! And, thank you for all the adventures we've been on together, both in China (Ergotou!) and here in the USA. The adventures on the mountains in Arizona and in the cities of China are some of my fondest memories!

Thank you Gerald Thomason in Oklahoma for the friendship, the knowledge and the additional information. Gerald has done a lot for the world of Korean Kung Fu with his studies and has written articles for Inside Kung Fu magazine on the art. Mr. Thomason provided some important information on the pioneers of Korean Kung Fu for this book.

And to his teacher, Sifu David Scott for your continued friendship over the years and for having me out at your school to observe you and your wonderful students!

Thank you to Grandmaster Kang Rhee for accepting me as a member of the World Black Belt Bureau and for the glowing compliments you gave to me each time I visited. You are a true martial arts grandmaster and one of the finest individuals I have ever met in the martial arts. You are truly inspirational!

ACKNOWLEDGEMENTS

Thank you to the late Grandmaster Byong Yil Choi for openly accepting me into your school and for sharing your knowledge and resources with me. Even though I only knew you for a few short years, those were some of the best years of my life. May you rest in peace and I hope your dojang in the sky is *filled* with eager students.

Thank you to the late Grandmaster Bong Soo Han for taking me on a fantastic journey in Hapkido and for allowing me to be one of your last students before the world lost a legend.

Thank you to Grandmaster Yong Sung Lee for opening your heart, your home and your school to me and for treating me like a brother. Thank you for being the coolest Korean I know. You have been a wonderful influence in my life and have helped me grow in so many ways.

Thank you to my wife, Debi for giving me the free time and the support to live the life of my dreams. You were the student that I had always hoped I would find one day and I owe ALL of my success to you! You are the best thing that ever happened to me!

Thank you to Master Choi Bok Kyu for inviting my wife and me out to meet you and learn from you. It's wonderful to know that there are others out there who research and give back to the martial arts community unselfishly the way that you have. You are my Korean brother and I am always there if you need me.

Thank you to everyone who has contacted me over the years to inquire about what I do. It's refreshing to know that there are at least a small group of traditionalists out there who care enough about our art to take the time to learn about it and keep it alive.

Thank you to Grandmaster Mike Shaw for keeping the art alive in Canada!

Thank you to my wonderful associate Sue Balcer of Just YourType.biz for helping me with the design and typesetting of my books. You're awesome!!

And, finally, thank you to my students for believing in me and for sticking with me through thick and thin. You guys make me who I am. Without you, I'd just be a guy dressed in pajamas swinging weapons around and looking crazy! Special thank you's to Matt Hampson, Ashley Furgason, and Matt Tucher for your years of loyalty and dedication. It is an honor to call you my students.

ACKNOWLEDGEMENTS

CHOI YOUNG PYO PERFORMING STRAIGHT SWORD FORM, 1984

DEBI THEROS, GRANDMASTER LEE JAE BONG, JAMES THEROS, KOREA 2008

FRONT SNAP KICK 2008

GRAINY PICTURE OF JOON P. CHOI, THE AUTHOR, AND YOUNG P. CHOI, 1983

GRANDMASTER HWANG JU HWAN 2011

GRANDMASTER HWANG JU HWAN BREAKS CEMENT TILES WITH BACK HAND STRIKE

Korean Kung Fu: The Chinese Connection

GRANDMASTER HWANG JU HWAN PERFORMING

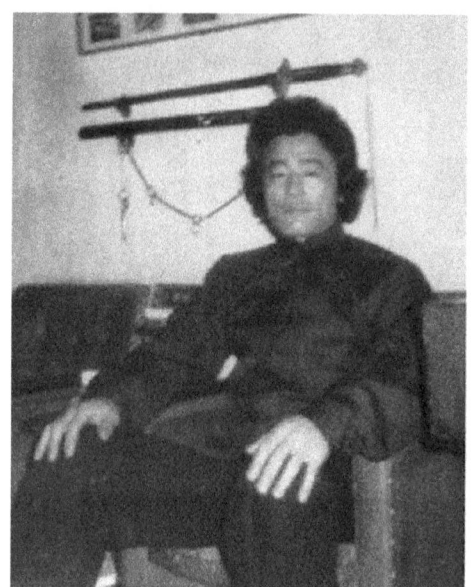

GRANDMASTER YOON HA DO (TEACHER OF GRANDMASTER HI SEUP NA, LEE JAE BONG)

JAMES THEROS (SIDE KICK 1993)

JAMES THEROS 3 SECTIONAL STAFF 2014

ACKNOWLEDGEMENTS

JAMES THEROS AND CHOI BYUNG YIL, 2004

JAMES THEROS AND GRANDMASTER LI JIN HENG, 1999

JAMES THEROS AND GRANDMASTER
YOUNG P. CHOI, 1999

JAMES THEROS AND GRANDMASTER YOUNG PYO CHOI
(IN HIS MODIFIED KUNG FU UNIFORM), 2003

Korean Kung Fu: The Chinese Connection

JAMES THEROS CHAIN WHIP 2014

JAMES THEROS POSES WITH TROPHY COLLECTION, 1999

JAMES THEROS IN KUNG FU CLASS WITH GRANDMASTER YOUNG PYO CHOI, 1998

JAMES THEROS PERFORMS LONG STAFF 2014

ACKNOWLEDGEMENTS

JAMES THEROS PRAYING MANTIS POSE 2014

JAMES THEROS QI GONG POSE, 1986

JAMES THEROS SIDE KICK 2002

JAMES THEROS SIDE KICK 1984

JAMES THEROS TAN TUI POSE 2014

Korean Kung Fu: The Chinese Connection

JAMES THEROS, HWANG JANG LEE (THE SILVER FOX), CHANG IL DO (BRUCE LAI)

KANG DUK MOO KWAN SCHOOL PATCH
(GIFT FROM LEE JAE BONG, KOREA 2008)

JAMES THEROS, SHAOLIN QUAN POSE

KUNG FU FLAG---GIFT FROM LEE JAE BONG, KOREA 2008

STAFF KICK, 1998

ACKNOWLEDGEMENTS

STAFF KICK, 2008

THE AUTHOR STANDING IN FRONT OF LEE DUK KANG'S DOJANG
IN SEOUL, KOREA, 2008

CPSIA information can be obtained
at www.ICGtesting.com
Printed in the USA
BVHW03s2234090718
521057BV00027B/41/P